What this Book is all about

This book is a follow up to "Fortigate Admin Pocket Guide ":

Following The basic administration and the creation of interfaces, policies, routes, and logs, we will now start to think as security warriors and inspect our traffic for viruses, malware, anomalies as Denial of service attacks and exploits

"Fortigate Security pocket guide", will walk you through the different techniques and capabilities of your firewall protecting against different attack vectors

Every chapter includes hands-on practices

It is written for **beginners and intermediate users**

The following book will help you to get around and feel cozy with your FortiGate firewall protecting against different attacks

Table Of Contents

What this Book is all about   2

Table Of Contents   4

Flow-Based Inspection   7

Your Fortigate Firewall operates in 2 main inspection modes   7

Proxy-Based Inspection   10

Anti Virus   15

Your Fortigate will scan for Viruses, using different techniques   16

Content Disarm and Reconstruct   21

Intrusion Prevention System   26

IPS Signatures   29

Configuring A Sensor   32

Fine Tune Your IPS Settings   37

set fail-open   39

"set database"   39

"Set engine count"   40

Optimizing Your IPS   40

Web Filter   44

Override a category   52

Web Filter optimization   54

Application Control   66

The order of the operation is quite significant !!!   68

Anomalies   82

Quarantine attackers   87

Web Application Firewall   91

Explicit Proxy   105

Proxy Auto-Config   111

Block IP Domains   117

Final Words   129

In my first book **"Fortigate Admin Pocket Guide"** you have learned how to configure your network interfaces, set up policy rules, and analyze logs

You have also learned how routing works, What are sessions on your fortigate firewall, how to see and analyze them using the command line
In this book, we will learn security concepts through the security profiles. Each security profile can be enabled on your policy according to your network needs

 **Security Profiles**

AntiVirus

Web Filter

DNS Filter

Application Control

Intrusion Prevention

Web Application Firewall

Flow-Based Inspection

Your Fortigate Firewall operates in 2 main inspection modes

- Flow-based
- Proxy-based

You can change the inspection mode on the policy page for each policy

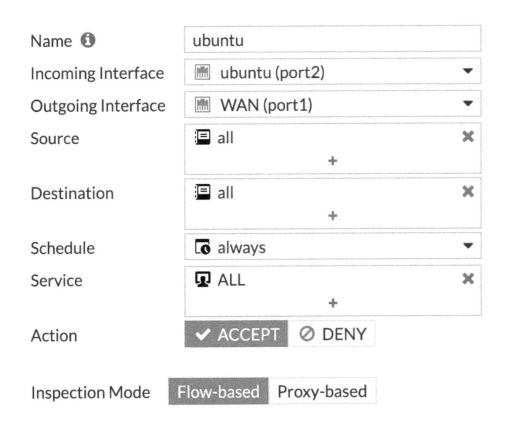

Let's look at what happens when you apply an antivirus profile in a flow-based mode. A flow-based inspection mode is used heavily in many use cases and is probably the one that you will use the most

let's assume that we have our host our fortigate. And there's the internet.

Whenever a host connects to a website or to any resource on the web fortigate doesn't interfere with the three-way handshake. The **TCP SYN**, the **TCP ACK,** and the **TCP SYN-ACK** go through our fortigate. And gets back to our host.

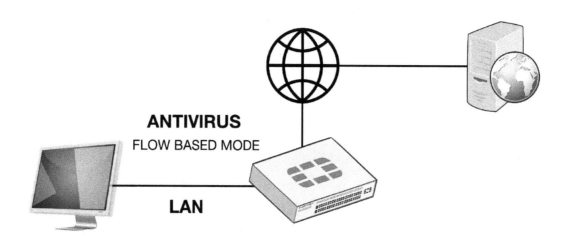

Fortigate only looks at the flow of packets, **Packet after Packet**. The same way as we see packets on Wireshark or other tools.

Fortigate actually caches the packets, but it lets them move to the other side. It doesn't buffer them and keeps them for internal scanning. It caches them and when the last packet of a file is received, then your fortigate will buffer it. It will not send it towards the destination until it finishes the scan.

If a virus is found, the last packet is dropped and the connection will reset

Proxy-Based Inspection

A Proxy-based inspection mode is much more strict, if you choose it, you will have more options in different security profiles, your scan will be much more granular, but, and that is a big BUT!!! , you will need to allocate much more resources for that operation

Again, you can change the inspection mode on the policy page

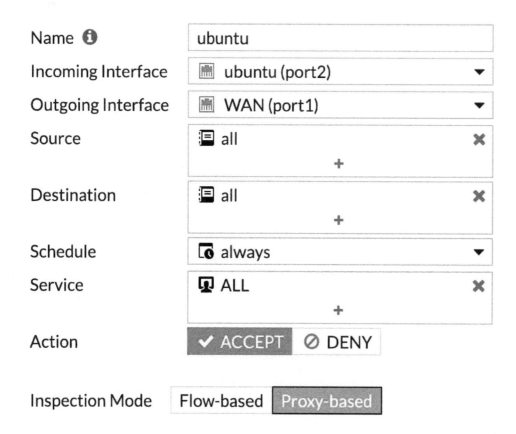

Proxy-based inspection works by buffering the whole file before it is sent to the host. Our host will have to wait for the inspection to end

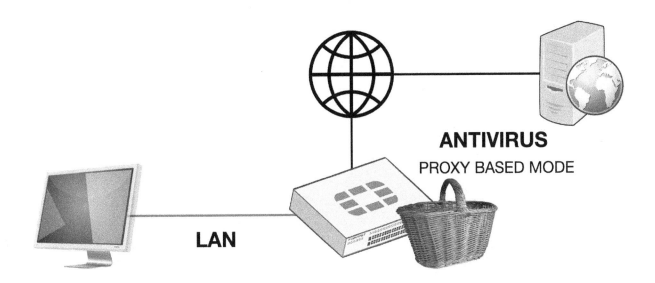

ANTIVIRUS
PROXY BASED MODE

LAN

When you use a proxy-based inspection, you will want to send packets to your host, to make sure that the connection doesn't time out

To do that, navigate to **policy and objects---protocol options**

There you will find different protocol options to play around with, one of them is the comfort clients options

Enable it

Protocol Port Mapping

Protocol			Port
HTTP	◖	any **Specify**	80
SMTP	◖	any **Specify**	25
POP3	◖	any **Specify**	110
IMAP	◖	any **Specify**	143
FTP	◖	any **Specify**	21
NNTP	◖	any **Specify**	119
MAPI	◖	135	
DNS	◖	53	
CIFS	◖	445	

Common Options

Comfort Clients	◖
Interval (seconds)	10 ⇕
Amount (bytes)	1

Once done, your fortigate will send packets in an interval and amount, that you will configure, so the other side host will not time out

A proxy-based mode is much more resource-intensive, But it gives you better results in finding out viruses. So if you prefer performance versus security then choose a flow-based mode that is suitable for most scenarios.

If you're not willing to sacrifice your security for anything, even performance, then use the **proxy-based** mode.

Anti Virus

Anti-virus is a database of virus signatures that are used to identify virus infections

during the scan, a virus must match a defined pattern called **a signature**

Signatures can be made of hashes, CRC, file attributes, binary values in different areas of the file, encryption keys, parts of code, and more

Your Fortigate will scan for Viruses, using different techniques

- Detects viruses based on pattern (signature match)
- **Grayware scan** - looks for adware, spyware (an unsolicited program that is being downloaded to your computer)
- **Heuristic** - based on probability (looks for anti-virus code that does suspicious things as modifying the registry or connects frequently to a botnet site … anything that is greater than a threshold). helps with zero-day viruses.

You can use your AntiVirus Profile, in either **Proxy or Flow-based mode**. As said Proxy is the most secure method but will consume more resources

Navigate to security profiles --- antivirus

You have predefined antivirus profiles, that you can already use, or create a new profile

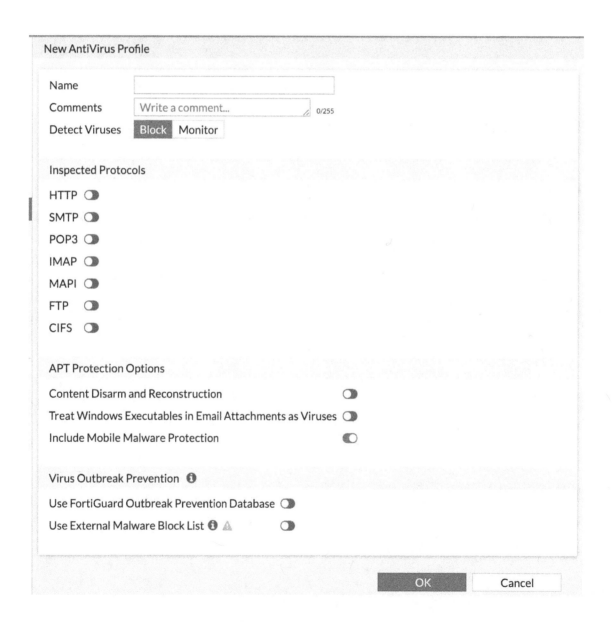

Here you will find the list of protocols that you want to inspect and some more advanced features as **CDR** that we will look into soon

Now the first thing that needs to be done is to choose your virus database, there are actually several of them

Let's open the CLI

"Config antivirus settings"
"Show full-configuration"

```
FortiGate-VM64 # config antivirus settings

FortiGate-VM64 (settings) # show full-configuration
config antivirus settings
    set default-db extended
    set grayware enable
    set override-timeout 0
end

FortiGate-VM64 (settings) #
```

If you write **"set default-db"** and press the TAB button, you will see, that you can change between different databases

```
FortiGate-VM64 (settings) # set default-db normal
```

```
FortiGate-VM64 (settings) # set default-db extended
```

```
FortiGate-VM64 (settings) # set default-db extreme
```

The **Extreme database** has (as its name suggests) the largest set of
signatures, new and legacy, the **Extended** includes more legacy signatures than
the **Normal**

Another option that you will want to make sure that it is enabled, is the **Grayware**
scan

```
FortiGate-VM64 (settings) # set grayware enable
```

Next, **Enable Heuristics**
To enable it, you will use another command

```
FortiGate-VM64 # config anFortiGate-VM64 # config antivirus heuristic

FortiGate-VM64 (heuristic) # set mode pass
```

But be cautious, a heuristic scan adds up to the amount of false-positive events.
using heuristics, you have 3 options:
- Disable
- Pass
- block

Since Antivirus consumes resources, you can use your fortigate hardware acceleration to offload the inspection process to the dedicated ASIC's of your firewall

Hardware acceleration works only on the flow-based inspection mode and you need to choose it based on the type of Asics that you have (CP or NP)

"config ips global"

"set cp-accel-mode"

If your model supports the NP processor

"set np-accel-mode"

```
FortiGate-VM64 # FortiGate-VM64 # config ips global

FortiGate-VM64 (global) # set cp-accel-mode
```

Content Disarm and **Reconstruct**

One of the nicest features of your fortigateAntivirus profile is the content disarm. It only works on a proxy-based mode. And what it does is actually stripping content from office files and PDF files.

We have dozens or hundreds of files that are sent every day over the email, which is the number one virus and malware attack surface.
 Sometimes you want to block that content up until it is being scanned by a FortiSandbox.

APT Protection Options

Content Disarm and Reconstruction

Original File Destination | FortiSandbox | File Quarantine | Discard |

Treat Windows Executables in Email Attachments as Viruses

Include Mobile Malware Protection

When setting up CDR, we can choose either to discard the embedded content or to send it to a **FortiSandbox** if you have one or your license includes this feature.

You can also choose which content to disarm and which not.

Let's create a new profile, name it **"disarm"**

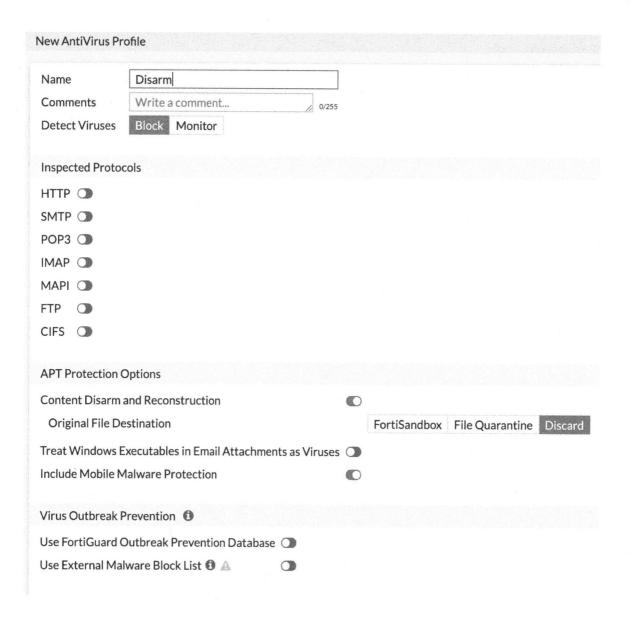

Save it

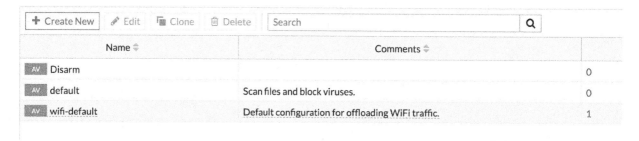

Open up your CLI and write:

"config antvirus profile"

"edit Disarm" (if you named your profile differently, just use the TAB to move between profiles

```
FortiGate-VM64 # config antivirus profile

FortiGate-VM64 (profile) # edit Disarm

FortiGate-VM64 (Disarm) #
```

Next, write **"config content-disarm"**

"show full-configuration "

And press enter

```
FortiGate-VM64 # FortiGate-VM64 # config antivirus profile

FortiGate-VM64 (profile) # edit Disarm

FortiGate-VM64 (Disarm) # config content-disarm

FortiGate-VM64 (content-disarm) # show full-configuration
config content-disarm
    set original-file-destination discard
    set office-macro enable
    set office-hylink enable
    set office-linked enable
    set office-embed enable
    set office-dde enable
    set office-action enable
    set pdf-javacode enable
    set pdf-embedfile enable
    set pdf-hyperlink enable
    set pdf-act-gotor enable
    set pdf-act-launch enable
    set pdf-act-sound enable
    set pdf-act-movie enable
    set pdf-act-java enable
    set pdf-act-form enable
    set cover-page enable
    set detect-only disable
end
```

You will see that you can set to enable or disable content disarm on specific files and specific formats.

You can, for example, enable it on macros and disable it on hyperlinks in a PDF.

```
FortiGate-VM64 (content-disarm) # set office-macro disable
```

CDR is great for zero-day viruses.

Intrusion Prevention System

Your IPS engine is probably the most important component of your firewall. It is used extensively in application control in antivirus and more security profiles.

Your IPS can distinguish between **Well-known attacks and Anomalies**

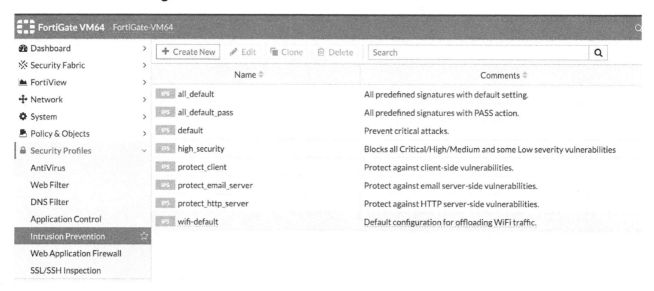

 When you configure your IPS sensor, you configure it towards a specific target either clients or servers, towards a specific operating system, either Mac Linux windows

Navigate to **intrusion prevention---Create New**

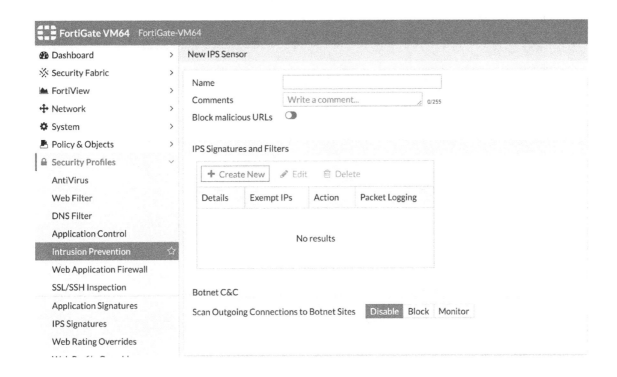

Name your IPS sensor

In IPS signatures and Filters, **Create New**

Here you will find the list of IPS signatures

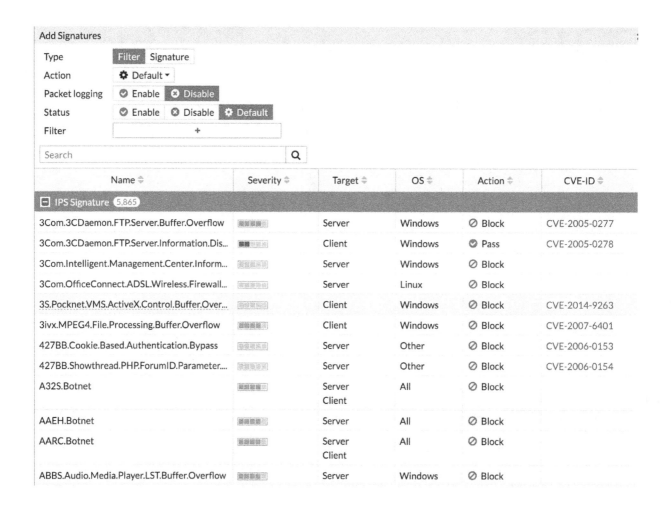

You can configure either specific or family of signatures or use the filter option, which allows you to configure pattern-based signatures, custom signatures, or rate based signatures

IPS Signatures

Signatures can be filtered based on

- **Target type**
- **Operating system**
- **Protocol**
- **Applications**

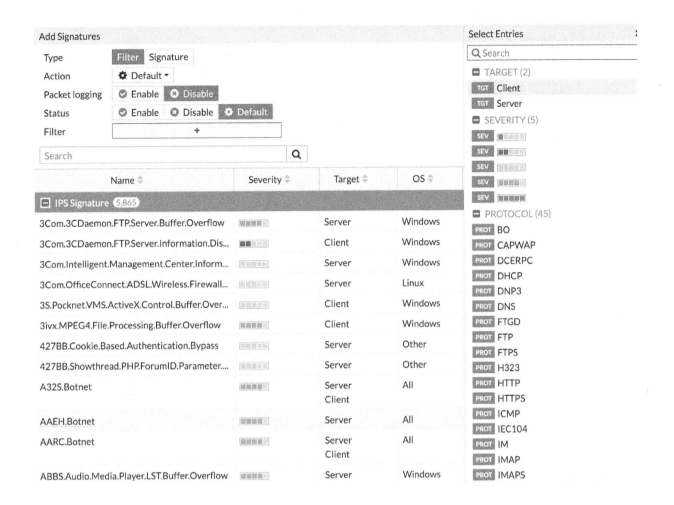

The best practice approach is to specify signatures based on your topology
Use signatures based on your operating system (Mac, Linux, Windows), your
targeted applications, or even for a specific set of protocols

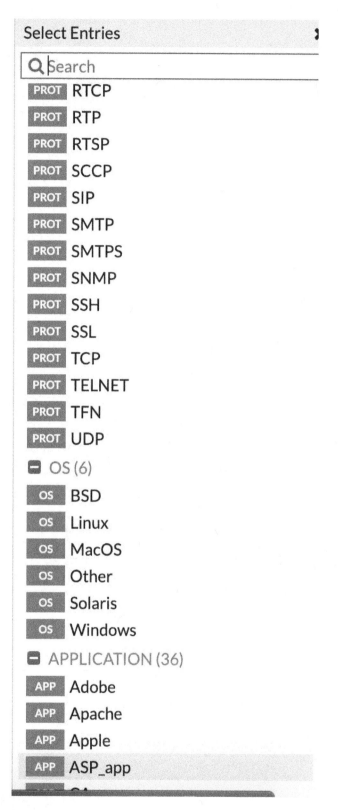

Select Entries

Search

PROT	RTCP
PROT	RTP
PROT	RTSP
PROT	SCCP
PROT	SIP
PROT	SMTP
PROT	SMTPS
PROT	SNMP
PROT	SSH
PROT	SSL
PROT	TCP
PROT	TELNET
PROT	TFN
PROT	UDP

OS (6)

OS	BSD
OS	Linux
OS	MacOS
OS	Other
OS	Solaris
OS	Windows

APPLICATION (36)

APP	Adobe
APP	Apache
APP	Apple
APP	ASP_app

Remember, your IPS is the most demanding resource of your fortigate

The attack surface itself can come from botnets. It can come from IoT devices, it can come from the cloud. Your IPS engine uses protocol decoders to look for different patterns to look for mismatch in the protocols themselves.

So let's look at how we set up an IPS sensor.

Configuring A Sensor

We have some default profiles already configured for us

Name ⇕	Comments ⇕
IPS all_default	All predefined signatures with default setting.
IPS all_default_pass	All predefined signatures with PASS action.
IPS default	Prevent critical attacks.
IPS high_security	Blocks all Critical/High/Medium and some Low severity vulnerabilities
IPS protect_client	Protect against client-side vulnerabilities.
IPS protect_email_server	Protect against email server-side vulnerabilities.
IPS protect_http_server	Protect against HTTP server-side vulnerabilities.
IPS wifi-default	Default configuration for offloading WiFi traffic.

let's create a new one. As said, we can choose between signatures and filter which are actually adding up signatures that have common behavior. So we can add signatures by their severity level, by the target they're after, by the protocol, or maybe the applications that you're running on your servers.

We will create a profile that is targeting servers, the severity level is high. The protocols that they're running are HTTP, HTTPS, and FTP, and the operating system is Windows.

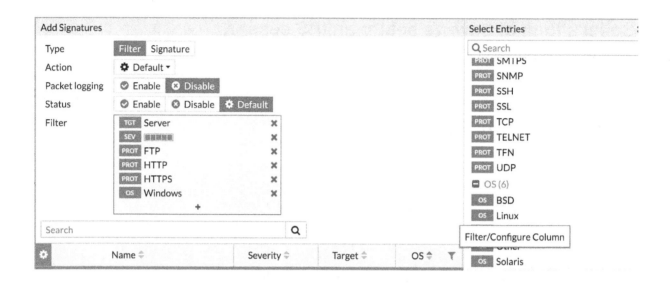

Those are the servers that we have in our organization, each signature has a default action, but let's set them all to block.

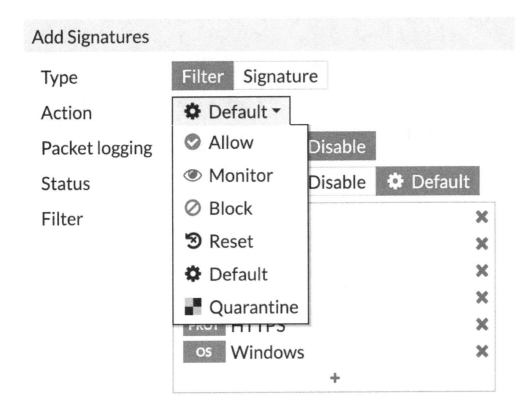

So anyone would build any intrusion that is aiming servers, running FTP, HTTP and HTTPS and Windows operating system, which have a severity level of high and more will be blocked.

New IPS Sensor

Name	webservers
Comments	Write a comment... 0/255
Block malicious URLs	⬤

IPS Signatures and Filters

+ Create New   ✏ Edit   🗑 Delete

Details	Exempt IPs	Action	Packet Logging
`TGT` ... `SEV` ... `PROT` ... `PROT` ... `+2`		⊘ Block	✖ Disabled

Botnet C&C

Scan Outgoing Connections to Botnet Sites   **Disable** | Block | Monitor

---

Now, we can also add up another criterion, which is applications, your organization may run different applications by IBM, HP, Cisco, and more. We will choose HP. So any application by HP that runs on your web server, will be also included in that IPS sensor.

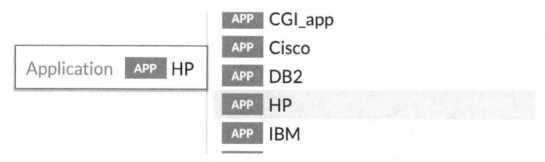

Now, we can set it up and apply our new sensor to our policy

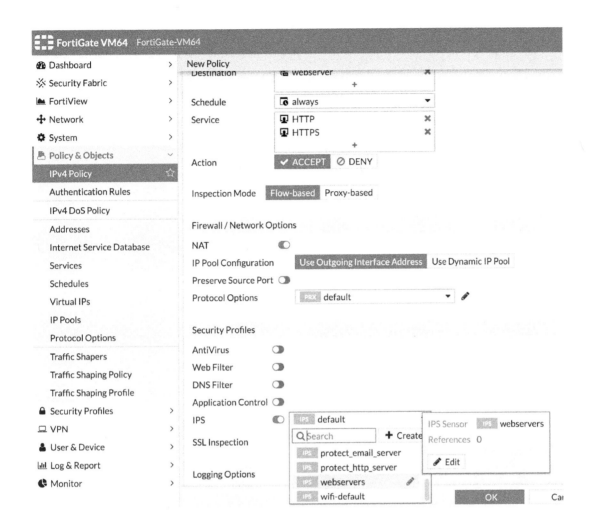

Dashboard >
Security Fabric >
FortiView >
Network >
System >
Policy & Objects ∨
  IPv4 Policy ☆
  Authentication Rules
  IPv4 DoS Policy
  Addresses
  Internet Service Database
  Services
  Schedules
  Virtual IPs
  IP Pools
  Protocol Options
  Traffic Shapers
  Traffic Shaping Policy
  Traffic Shaping Profile
Security Profiles >
VPN >
User & Device >
Log & Report >
Monitor >

New Policy

Destination   webserver   ✕
                                    +
Schedule   always   ▼
Service   HTTP   ✕
                       HTTPS   ✕
                                    +
Action   ✔ ACCEPT   ⊘ DENY

Inspection Mode   Flow-based   Proxy-based

Firewall / Network Options
NAT   ⬤
IP Pool Configuration Use Outgoing Interface Address   Use Dynamic IP Pool
Preserve Source Port   ⬤
Protocol Options   PRX default   ▼   ✏

Security Profiles
AntiVirus   ⬤
Web Filter   ⬤
DNS Filter   ⬤
Application Control   ⬤
IPS   ⬤   IPS default

SSL Inspection   🔍 Search   + Create

Logging Options   IPS protect_email_server
                                 IPS protect_http_server
                                 IPS webservers   ✏
                                 IPS wifi-default

IPS Sensor   IPS webservers
References   0

✏ Edit

OK   Cai

Fine Tune Your IPS Settings

Whenever there is an issue with the IPS such as CPU spikes, or maybe your fortigate gets into a conserve mode, you will need to analyze the issue
You can adjust your IPS settings by using the command line.
Let's open the CLI and write down

"config IPS global"
"show full config"

```
FortiGate-VM64 # config ips global

FortiGate-VM64 (global) # show full-configuration
config ips global
    set fail-open disable
    set database regular
    set traffic-submit disable
    set anomaly-mode continuous
    set session-limit-mode heuristic
    set intelligent-mode enable
    set socket-size 128
    set engine-count 0
    set sync-session-ttl enable
    set skype-client-public-ipaddr ''
    set deep-app-insp-timeout 0
    set deep-app-insp-db-limit 0
    set exclude-signatures industrial
end
```

Using the **"show full config"** you will see all the different settings.
The settings that are the most relevant are:

set fail-open

```
set fail-open disable
```

By default, it is disabled, which actually means that if your IPS engine for any reason, collapses due to resources, or buffer size, and so on, the traffic will be dropped. If it is enabled, the traffic will still flow without inspection

"set database"

You actually have two databases the first one is **Regular** which includes all the well-known and the latest anomalies and intrusions

The **extended database** includes all of that and the legacy ones, it is a bigger database so performance can drop a bit.

```
FortiGate-VM64 # config ips global

FortiGate-VM64 (global) # set database regular
```

Another setting that is important is the **socket size**. This socket size is actually the buffer size. The default size differs between models. And you can set up an integer between one mega and 64 mega.

"Set engine count"

There are several fortigate models. Most of them are from the high-end models that actually support several IPS engines. So if your fortigate supports several engines, you can set the count to more than one

Another setting is the **"set-skype-client-public-IP-addr"** is the place where you set up your public IP addresses in your network that will receive Skype session that will help you fortigate to identify Skype properly

Optimizing Your IPS

There are other places, that will help you to diagnose your IPS situation and impact the overall performance of your fortigate

On your CLI write the following command:

"Diag test application ipsmonitor"

```
FortiGate-VM64 # diag test application ipsmonitor

IPS Engine Test Usage:

    1: Display IPS engine information
    2: Toggle IPS engine enable/disable status
    3: Display restart log
    4: Clear restart log
    5: Toggle bypass status
    6: Submit attack characteristics now
   10: IPS queue length
   11: Clear IPS queue length
   12: IPS L7 socket statistics
   13: IPS session list
   14: IPS NTurbo statistics
   15: IPSA statistics
   18: Display session info cache
   19: Clear session info cache
   21: Reload FSA malicious URL database
   22: Reload whitelist URL database
   24: Display Flow AV statistics
   25: Reset Flow AV statistics
   27: Display Flow urlfilter statistics
   28: Reset Flow urlfilter statistics
   29: Display global Flow urlfilter statistics
   30: Reset global Flow urlfilter statistics
   32: Reload certificate blacklist database
   96: Toggle IPS engines watchdog timer
   97: Start all IPS engines
   98: Stop all IPS engines
   99: Restart all IPS engines and monitor
```

Press enter, you will see a list of options that you can choose from

Some of the most important ones

option number 5 "**toggle bypass status**"

If you write down the command again " **diag test application ipsmonitor 5**" you will actually enable bypass or disable bypass. if you're still having an issue with your CPU, after enabling the bypass, (by disabling, your IPS will still work. But it will not inspect traffic) then you're probably having issues with network congestion, or your fortigate is not up to the task, there's too much traffic.

```
FortiGate-VM64 # diag test application ipsmonitor 5

FortiGate-VM64 #
```

But if you're disabling bypass,(your IPS still works and inspects traffic) and you're still having issues with the CPU. That means that you probably have an issue with your IPS engine.

Option number 99 - turn on or turn off your IPS, you can do it using option 99 "**Diag test application ipsmonitor 99**"

And if you want to start your IPS engine, again, you can use option 99 that will actually restart all your IPS engine operations.

```
FortiGate-VM64 # diag test application ipsmonitor 99
restarting ipsmonitor
```

Other commands to optimize your IPS operations are done in the global configuration of your IPS

"config IPS global"

"set intelligent-mode"

```
FortiGate-VM64 # config ips global

FortiGate-VM64 (global) # set intelligent-mode enable
```

One of the most important options that you can play around with is the intelligent mode. Currently, it is by default enabled. The intelligent mode actually means that your fortigate IPS engine will look at the session itself. It will not scan by default every byte in this session, it will look and it will use heuristics and other techniques to choose if to scan the whole session or to stop scanning the session traffic upon recognizing that it is secure enough.

So be sure that you're using the intelligent mode that will actually offload CPU resources memory resources from your fortigate

Web **Filter**

Probably one of the most used and popular security profiles, in any scenario.

When you use a web filter, it actually comes to life after the following steps:

- Host requests to get into a website
- It goes through a DNS request and a DNS response.
- Then it starts the session itself using TCP SYN, SYN-ACK that comes back from our web server, and ACK that is sent back from our
- And then our host asks for resources using HTTP GET.
- Gets a response back from the web server with the HTTP 200 message (OK, everything is good).
- Our web filter actually starts to work.

Navigate to security profiles

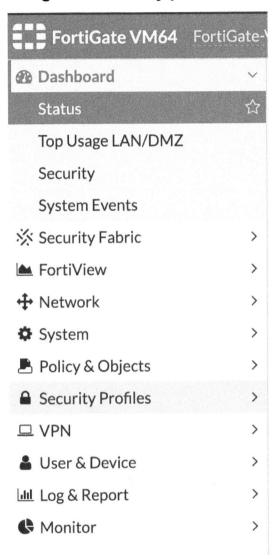

Choose Web Filter

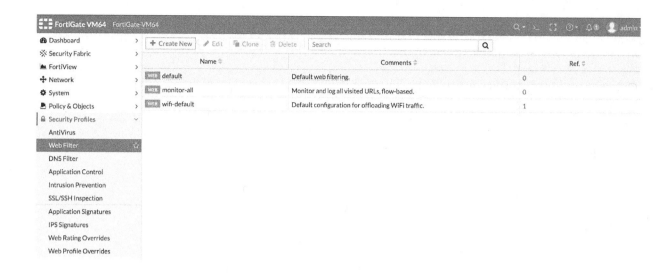

As the name applies, that is the filter that will allow you to monitor or restrict access from our users to different resources on the web.

Depending on your firmware, your fortigate will come with several pre-configured profiles.

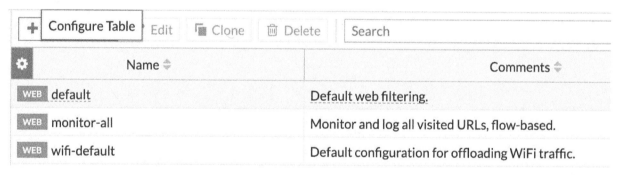

- The first one is the default profile
- The second one is the monitor all profiles, which will actually log any URL that your user visits.
- And the third one is the Wi-Fi default profile

Web filter profile will work under both the proxy and the flow-based inspection modes.

When you create a new profile, we will see that we have proxy only features.

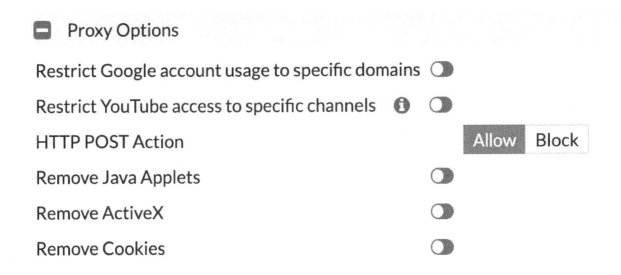

Once you finished configuring your profile, you will use it and apply it to your policy.

So let's move over to our profile. And let's create a new profile. And name it "test profile".

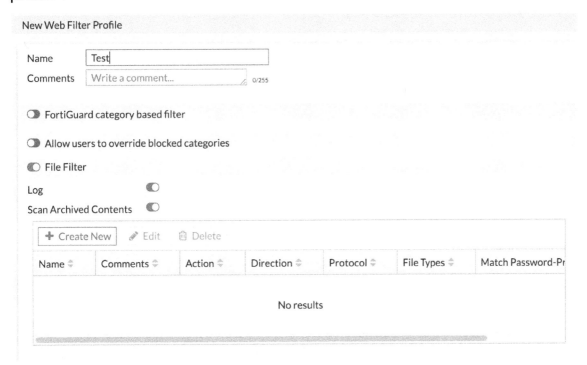

The first thing that you will see is the **FortiGuard** category based filter.

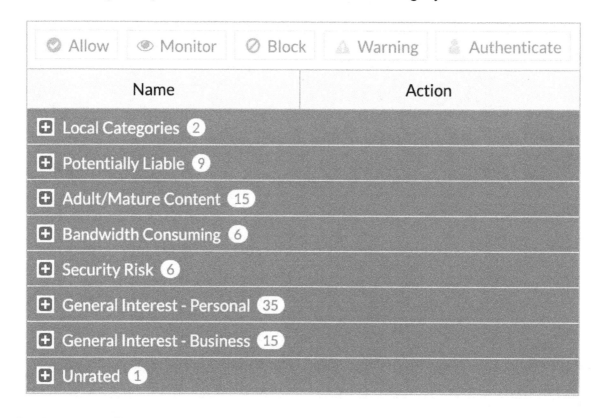

Fortinet actually sorted millions of websites of URL resources, and categorize them under different categories.

Each category can be enabled, and used with different actions - just right click on the action and you will see a prompt of different Actions, that you can use

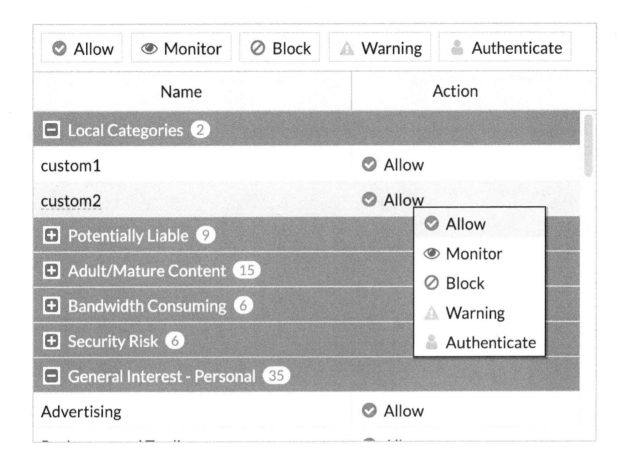

The **Actions**

Besides the allowed action, you will find the following actions:

Blocked - Traffic will be blocked

Monitored - allowing the users to go to the tree source, but your fortigate will log any event

Warning - you can also use a warning page in specific intervals

Authenticate - allow different groups to use their credentials to get into that resource.

Edit Filter						Select Entries
						🔍 Search
Warning Interval	0	hour(s)	5	minute(s)	0	▦ Guest-group
Selected User Groups		+				🖳 SSO_Guest_Users

OK   Cancel

Override **a category**

You can create different actions for different categories on your web filter.
But you can also override them for specific users.
So let's create a new security profile **"block news"**

And let's set up the action for new sites to block and then override it using our web ratings override

We can override with specific groups, but this time we will do it generally
The idea is to choose a news web site such as cnn.com and to change its category, instead of **general interest --- news** that is blocked now, to another category that is allowed
Move to **web rating overrides**

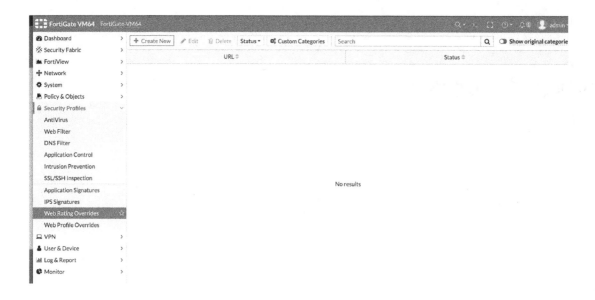

Create a new override

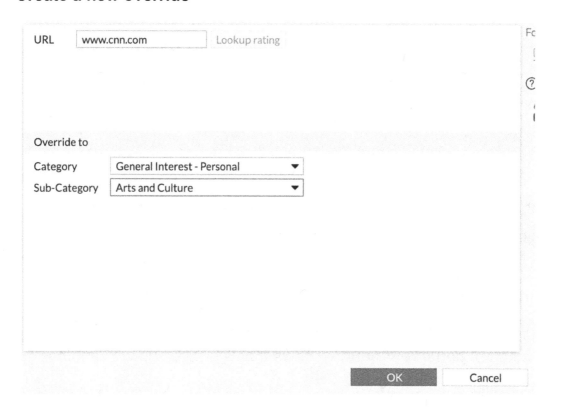

And there just enter the URL that you want to exclude from the blocked category and change its category and subcategory to an allowed one

Web Filter optimization

web filter seems to be the most used security profile on a fortigate firewall.

Your fortigate is in a constant dialogue with FortiGuard servers, one example is when using web categories.

There are dozens of categories. each time your fortigate asks for different categories rating, it saves the results in a cache.
This cache has a session Time To Live. If you want to make your fortigate performance better, you will need to make that cache stay for a longer time. How you do so using the command line.
So let's use the **"config system fortiGuard"**

```
FortiGate-VM64 (fortiguard) # show full-configuration
config system fortiguard
    set protocol https
    set port 8888
    set load-balance-servers 1
    set auto-join-forticloud disable
    set update-server-location usa
    set sandbox-region ''
    set fortiguard-anycast disable
    set antispam-force-off disable
    set antispam-cache enable
    set antispam-cache-ttl 1800
    set antispam-cache-mpercent 2
    set antispam-timeout 7
    set outbreak-prevention-force-off disable
    set outbreak-prevention-cache enable
    set outbreak-prevention-cache-ttl 300
    set outbreak-prevention-cache-mpercent 2
    set outbreak-prevention-timeout 7
    set webfilter-force-off disable
    set webfilter-cache enable
    set webfilter-cache-ttl 3600
    set webfilter-timeout 15
    set sdns-server-ip "208.91.112.220"
    set sdns-server-port 53
```

And now let's set the web filter cache. First, we will make it enabled if it is for any reason not enabled,

and then we will set the Cache Time To Live. to 4800 seconds. default is 3600.

```
FortiGate-VM64 (fortiguard) # set webfilter-cache enable

FortiGate-VM64 (fortiguard) # set webfilter-cache-ttl 4800
```

So we are actually setting the cache for much longer.

Blocking Files

Another great feature of a web filter is its ability to block the download of files in different file formats. This feature was once part of the DLP security profile, but now it actually landed in the web filter part

Under scan archived contents, you will find the option to block files, just click on the **Create New**

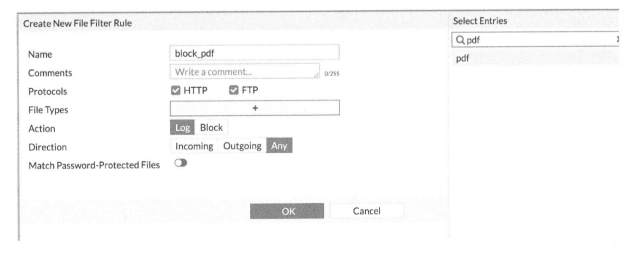

Name your filter

We will name it Block_pdf

Set your **protocol options**, either HTTP or FTP

And choose the file type, that you wish to block

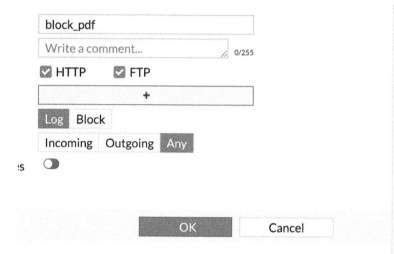

We will choose Pdf

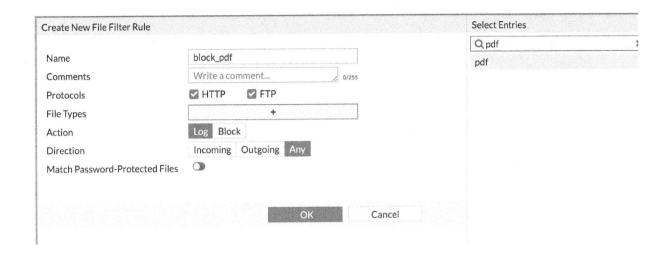

You can also choose if to block any attempt to download the files, or just to log the event

Another option is the direction of the traffic, for best results choose **Any**

Other Options

When you scroll to the bottom of the web filter security profile, you will see that you have other very interesting options, some of them will require that you will use the deep SSL inspection as in "Log al search keywords" where you can actually see search phrases that are used by your employees on search engines such as google

Search Engines

Enforce 'Safe Search' on Google, Yahoo!, Bing, Yandex ⬭

Restrict YouTube Access ⬭

Log all search keywords ⬭

Static URL Filter

Block invalid URLs ⬭

URL Filter ⬭

Block malicious URLs discovered by FortiSandbox ⬭

Content Filter ⬭

Rating Options

Allow websites when a rating error occurs ⬭

Rate URLs by domain and IP Address ⬭

Rate images by URL ⬮

Another very important option that is used heavily is the URL filter, here you can block, allow and monitor specific URLs. just enable it and you will have the option to create a **URL Filter**

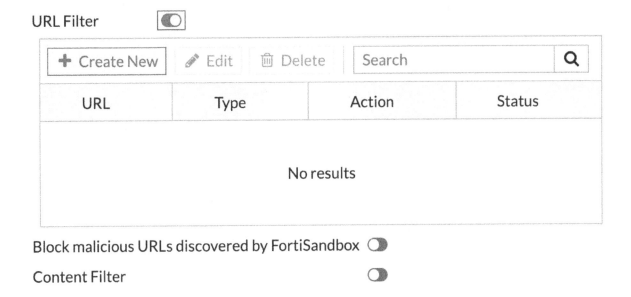

Create New

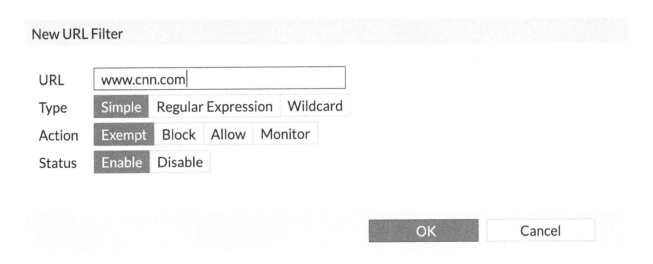

You can enter the URL as is, using the simple method, which is quite simple, but you can also use regular expression and wildcards for greater control

Wildcard

The wildcard is used to represent one or more characters. The most used character is the asterisk (*), which actually means "everything "

The best way to explain wildcard is the following

We are asked to block the following sites :

www.example.com

www.photos.example.com

www.example.org

If we would do it using the simple method, we would need to create 3 URL filters

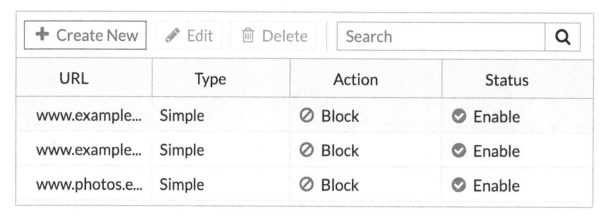

URL	Type	Action	Status
www.example...	Simple	⊘ Block	✓ Enable
www.example...	Simple	⊘ Block	✓ Enable
www.photos.e...	Simple	⊘ Block	✓ Enable

Another way which more practical is to use a wildcard in the following manner

New URL Filter

URL	*.example.*
Type	Simple	Regular Expression	**Wildcard**
Action	**Exempt**	Block	Allow	Monitor
Status	**Enable**	Disable

OK   Cancel

By using an asterisk before example and after it, Everything will be matched

Regular Expression

A regular expression is used heavily in different coding languages to find different text patterns. we will not get into the full syntax, it's not the purpose of this book, but let's play around with the following example :

We need to match three domains and two top-level domains (TLD) in one regular expression.

Our domains are: **cnn.com forbes.com and fox.org**
To play around with regular expression, I highly recommend using the regex101.com web app

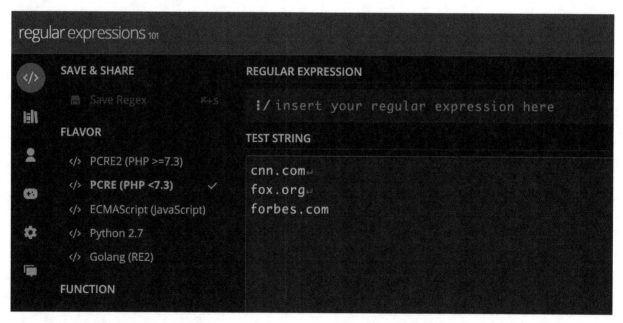

Let's open parentheses, and write down CNN and the **or (|)** sign.

Now let's write down Forbes and another **or** (|) sign, and Fox. Now let's close the parentheses.

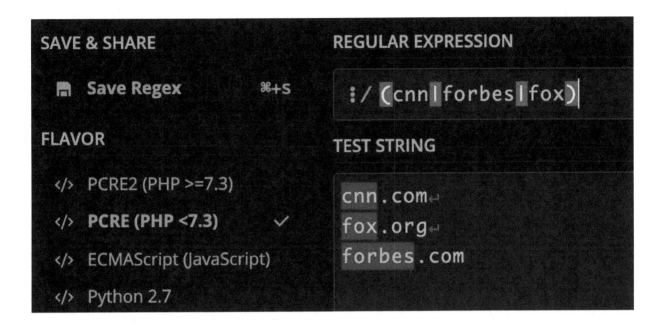

That's a good start

The **Dot** symbol in a regular expression means any character, so we will escape it using the backslash and then the dot character.

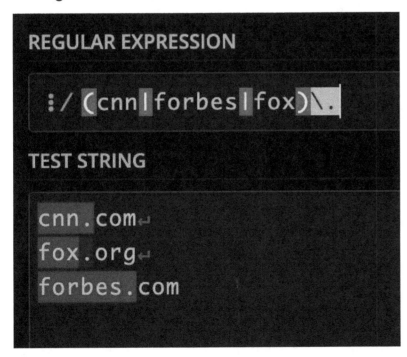

Alright, so now, we have the domain and the dot character

And now we only have the TLD. So we'll open new parentheses.
and We will write inside com or org and close the parentheses

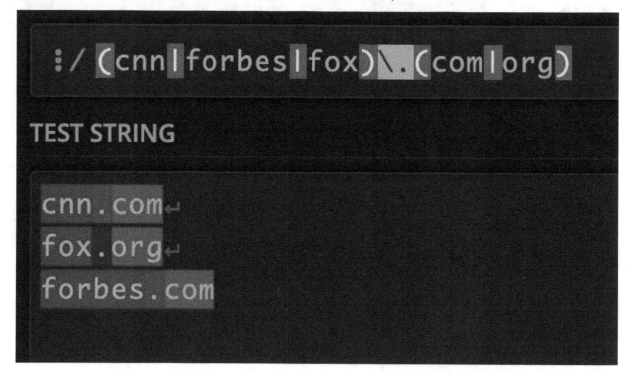

And we have a full match.

Now, you can take the code, you wrote and paste it in our URL filter.

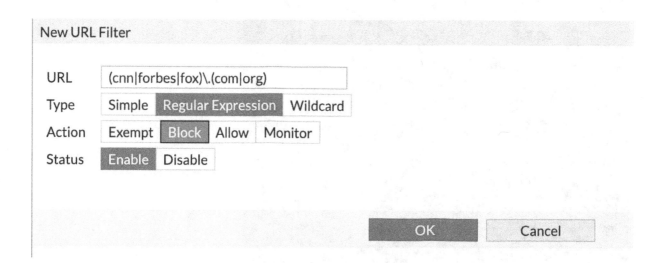

Application Control

Application control scans your traffic your network traffic for applications that you wish to control. It does so, using the IPS intrusion prevention system engine and its protocol decoders.

Application control can work in a proxy and a flow-based mode.

Usually, it will work in flow-based mode, as it relies heavily on the IPS

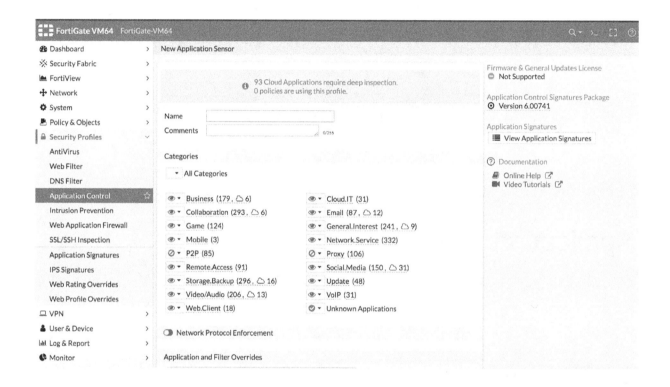

Application control detects new applications using signatures. the app DB provides details of signatures based on categories, risk, popularity (for example ' signatures of different proxy apps, in the proxy category)

There are 2 main places that you will want to make changes

- The categories - application categories
- The application and filter override

The order of the operation is quite significant !!!

The first thing that your fortigate scans are the application override where you add up your own predefined signatures or filter signatures based on behavior, protocol, popularity, application type, and more

Application and Filter Overrides

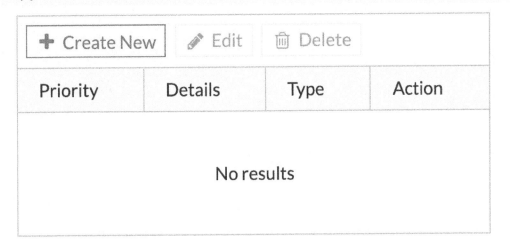

Specific signatures

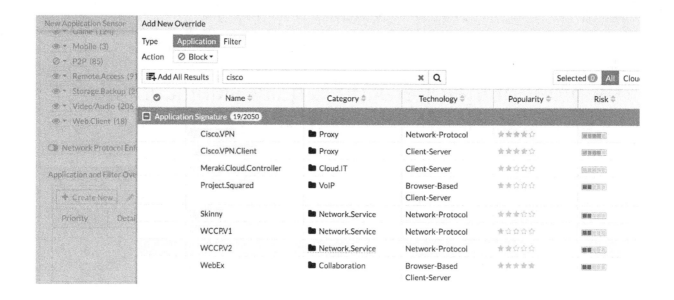

Common behavior signatures

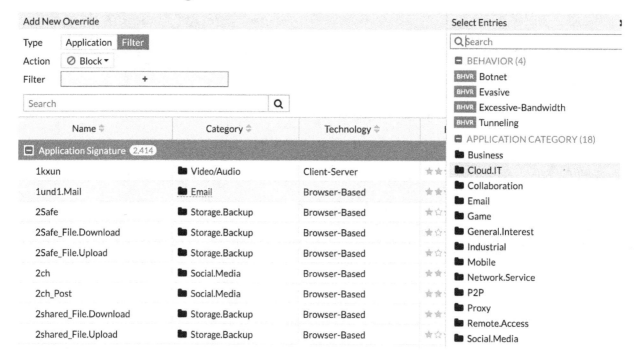

The next thing your fortigate does is inspecting different categories.

if you wish to block categories, such as remote access

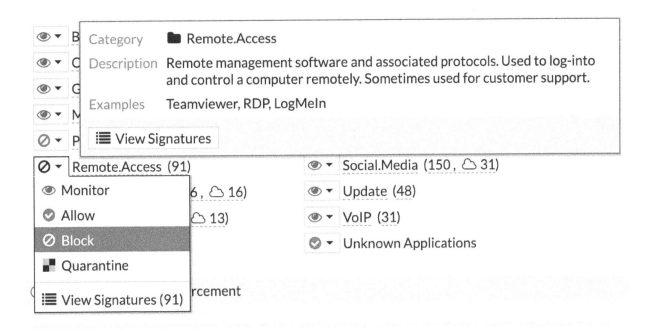

And yet you wish to enable a specific remote app, such as Teamviewer

you can do it

Let's just select every Teamviewer signatures, add them, and set the action to

allow

Fortigate will start by scanning application override, it will see that the

Teamviewer is allowed, and then it will move to categories where remote apps

are blocked.

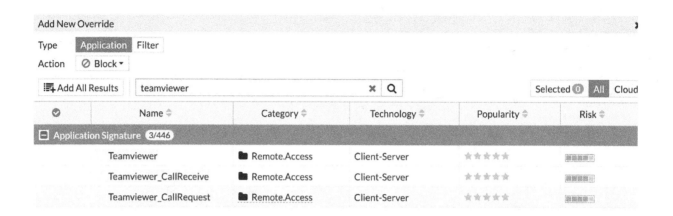

Doing so, Teamviewer will still work, while any other remote app will be blocked

When the IPS engine finds a match to an application, it tells your fortigate that it found an application ID number. Fortinet has a huge database of applications. Each one has its own ID.

 If you wish to see the different IDs for the different application, you use the CLI:

"config application list"
"edit 0"
 "config entries"
"edit 0"
"set application?"

```
FortiGate-VM64 # config apFortiGate-VM64 # config application list

FortiGate-VM64 (list) # edit 0
new entry '0' added

FortiGate-VM64 (0) # config entries

FortiGate-VM64 (entries) # edit 0
new entry '0' added

FortiGate-VM64 (0) # set application
ID              Select application ID
38614           1kxun
29025           1und1.Mail
36322           2Safe
36324           2Safe_File.Download
36323           2Safe_File.Upload
17534           2ch
17535           2ch_Post
31236           2shared_File.Download
31237           2shared_File.Upload
16284           3PC
35703           4Sync
35740           4Sync_File.Upload
16616           4shared
35760           4shared_File.Download
34742           4shared_File.Upload
35096           6cn_Search.Music
38923           8tracks
17045           9PFS
39431           9gag
26378           24im
28325           51.Com_BBS
28426           51.Com_Games
--More--            28323           51.Com_Mail
28387           51.Com_Music
28378           51.Com_Posting
28374           51.Com_Webdisk
36373           115Disk_File.Download
36374           115Disk_File.Upload
```

Now you can scroll between the different applications and their ID.

Remember, the Application control profile is not enabled globally on your firewall. Whenever you create an application sensor, name it and then use it in your different policies and the application sensor will be available only through that policy alone.

Whenever you as an administrator block an application, don't forget your users deserves an explanation of why that application was blocked.
So for an HTTP-based application, you can use the replacement messages (bottom page -options) for an HTTP-based application. make sure that it is enabled.

Options

Block applications detected on non-default ports ⓘ ⬤

Allow and Log DNS Traffic ⬤

QUIC ⓘ | Allow | Block |

Replacement Messages for HTTP-based Applications ⬤

When you enable it, your users will get a block page that will include the following information:

- The signature that detected the application
- The signatures category(remote access, peer to peer)
- The URL that was specifically blocked
- The client source - the IP address of the client
- The server's destination.
- Fortigate hostname and the UID of the policy that was governing the traffic.

Including Fortigate hostname is good in networks that have many fortigate devices, you can look up at the hostname of the fortigate and tell which fortigate actually blocked the traffic.

Application signatures

App signatures are organized by category, technology, and risk, they can be viewed using the view signatures that is to the right of your app control page

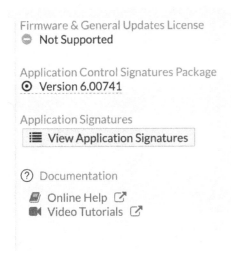

Firmware & General Updates License
⊖ Not Supported

Application Control Signatures Package
⊙ Version 6.00741

Application Signatures
≣ View Application Signatures

⑦ Documentation
📕 Online Help ↗
🎥 Video Tutorials ↗

Deep SSL Inspection

All cloud applications require you to enable deep SSL inspection on your policy in order to recognize them. These apps can be recognized using the padlock icon beside them, which means that their traffic is encrypted

Security Profiles

AntiVirus	⬤
Web Filter	⬤
DNS Filter	⬤
Application Control	⬤ APP block-high-risk ▼ ✏
IPS	⬤
SSL Inspection ⚠	SSL deep-inspection ▼ ✏
Mirror SSL Traffic to Interfaces	⬤

Denial of Service

IPV4 policies are not the only policies that can be configured on Your Fortigate firewall. One type of policy that you can configure is the DoS policy, where you protect your network from anomalies

DoS

One of the key principles of the CIA triad model (a theoretical model that describes, 3 key components that must be kept to keep your system secure) is Availability, which is keeping your systems up.

 A DoS attack purpose is usually to overwhelm your servers and make them unavailable

There are dozens of Dos attacks, that are happening all the time

Protecting your network from denial of service is probably one of the major tasks of your IPS engine.

let's create a Denial of Service policy.

Navigate to **Policy & objects---IPV4 Dos policy**

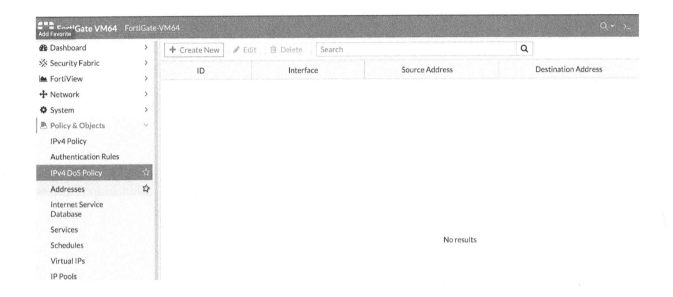

Create New

New Policy

Incoming Interface	▼	
Source Address	+	
Destination Address	+	
Service	+	

L3 Anomalies

Name	Logging	Action	Threshold
		Disable Block Monitor	
ip_src_session	⬤	Disable Block Monitor	5000
ip_dst_session	⬤	Disable Block Monitor	5000

L4 Anomalies

Name	Logging	Action	Threshold
		Disable Block Monitor	
tcp_syn_flood	⬤	Disable Block Monitor	2000
tcp_port_scan	⬤	Disable Block Monitor	1000
tcp_src_session	⬤	Disable Block Monitor	5000

We will configure the **incoming interface** which is usually the WAN interface,

Source address can be All

The **destination address** can also be All unless you want to protect a specific subnet.

Service is ALL

You can see that you have different anomalies that you can protect from, either
layer 3 anomalies and layer 4 anomalies

Anomaly	Toggle	Action			Threshold
tcp_syn_flood	◯	Disable	Block	Monitor	2000
tcp_port_scan	◯	Disable	Block	Monitor	1000
tcp_src_session	◯	Disable	Block	Monitor	5000
tcp_dst_session	◯	Disable	Block	Monitor	5000
udp_flood	◯	Disable	Block	Monitor	2000
udp_scan	◯	Disable	Block	Monitor	2000
udp_src_session	◯	Disable	Block	Monitor	5000
udp_dst_session	◯	Disable	Block	Monitor	5000
icmp_flood	◯	Disable	Block	Monitor	250
icmp_sweep	◯	Disable	Block	Monitor	100
icmp_src_session	◯	Disable	Block	Monitor	300
icmp_dst_session	◯	Disable	Block	Monitor	1000
sctp_flood	◯	Disable	Block	Monitor	2000
sctp_scan	◯	Disable	Block	Monitor	1000
sctp_src_session	◯	Disable	Block	Monitor	5000
sctp_dst_session	◯	Disable	Block	Monitor	5000

Each anomaly can be logged and in the middle of the table, you have different actions to choose from, either to block the traffic or to monitor

On the right side, you will find the **recommended threshold** for each anomaly, but you will need to configure the threshold based on your network topology, so get familiar with your network baseline.

Anomalies

Layer 3 - IP source session - That is if the number of concurrent IP connections from one source IP address exceeds the Configure threshold value. If so, the action you configured is executed

Layer 3 - IP destination session - That is if the number of concurrent IP connections to one destination IP exceeds the configured threshold value, then you also have an alert and the action is executed.

Moving to Layer 4 anomalies

TCP SYN flood is the classic denial of service attack, where an attacker sends a TCP SYN packets but doesn't respond to the TCP ACK sent by the victim. in this case. So if a server is a victim, will use resources as buffer memory waiting for the answer that will never come

As you can see you have a threshold of 2000, so if you have more than 2000 packets per second towards one source IP, then you will be alerted

TCP Port Scan - done by tools such as Nmap to scan the network for open and closed ports. if you have more than 1000 packets that are sent to one destination address, then it triggers the action.

Once you configure your sensor, just apply it to the policy itself and be aware of false-positive events since those anomalies can happen from time to time and not only due to denial of service attack.

Let's create another denial of service policy and this time we will protect our gateway interface from another anomaly which is the ICMP Flood attack

New Policy

Incoming Interface	▦ WAN (port1) ▼
Source Address	▤ all ✕
	+
Destination Address	▤ all ✕
	+
Service	🖵 ALL ✕
	+

If we will try to ping our gateway, Everything goes well, the rate is very slow, usually, 1 packet per second, the size of the packet is 56 bytes

```
Last login: Tue Jan 19 23:45:59 on ttys000
[ofershmueli@ofers-MacBook-Pro-1584 ~ % ping 192.168.1.1
PING 192.168.1.1 (192.168.1.1): 56 data bytes
64 bytes from 192.168.1.1: icmp_seq=0 ttl=64 time=2.078 ms
64 bytes from 192.168.1.1: icmp_seq=1 ttl=64 time=2.511 ms
64 bytes from 192.168.1.1: icmp_seq=2 ttl=64 time=2.619 ms
64 bytes from 192.168.1.1: icmp_seq=3 ttl=64 time=3.078 ms
64 bytes from 192.168.1.1: icmp_seq=4 ttl=64 time=2.118 ms
64 bytes from 192.168.1.1: icmp_seq=5 ttl=64 time=1.932 ms
64 bytes from 192.168.1.1: icmp_seq=6 ttl=64 time=2.969 ms
64 bytes from 192.168.1.1: icmp_seq=7 ttl=64 time=1.963 ms
64 bytes from 192.168.1.1: icmp_seq=8 ttl=64 time=2.645 ms
64 bytes from 192.168.1.1: icmp_seq=9 ttl=64 time=2.677 ms
```

But then again, we can many tools available free on the internet, to conduct a denial of service attack against our server, you can even use the hping tool available in Linux or the regular terminal on the Mac, with the following command Sudo Ping -f 192.168.1.1

-f stands for flood, your Mac will send hundreds and thousands of ICMP packets towards the destination

```
ofershmueli@ofers-MacBook-Pro-1584 ~ % sudo ping -f 192.168.1.1
Password:
PING 192.168.1.1 (192.168.1.1): 56 data bytes
..Request timeout for icmp_seq 98
..Request timeout for icmp_seq 671
..Request timeout for icmp_seq 675
..Request timeout for icmp_seq 1421
..Request timeout for icmp_seq 2615
..Request timeout for icmp_seq 3774
..Request timeout for icmp_seq 3781
.Request timeout for icmp_seq 3782
..Request timeout for icmp_seq 5107
.Request timeout for icmp_seq 5108
..Request timeout for icmp_seq 6677
..Request timeout for icmp_seq 8361
..Request timeout for icmp_seq 8374
..Request timeout for icmp_seq 10083
..Request timeout for icmp_seq 11833
..Request timeout for icmp_seq 13661
..Request timeout for icmp_seq 15517
..Request timeout for icmp_seq 15535
..Request timeout for icmp_seq 16406
..Request timeout for icmp_seq 17295
.Request timeout for icmp_seq 17296
.Request timeout for icmp_seq 17297
.^C
--- 192.168.1.1 ping statistics ---
19228 packets transmitted, 19205 packets received, 0.1% packet loss
round-trip min/avg/max/stddev = 1.328/4.980/43.354/2.761 ms
ofershmueli@ofers-MacBook-Pro-1584 ~ %
```

As you can see, almost 20000 packets were sent in about 5 seconds

What Do We Do?

In our Policy, Move over to layer 4 anomalies. ICMP flood.

enable it and set the action to **block**

Let's set the threshold to **20 ICMP packets per second.**

The effect of that threshold is as follows: once someone tries to ping our WAN with more than 20 packets the ICMP traffic will be blocked. Up until then, he will get an ICMP reply, but once our IPS engine recognized that the threshold has been crossed. The traffic will be blocked.

Quarantine attackers

If you're suffering from a denial of service attack, (ICMP flood SYN flood attack, and so on) your IPS alerts you and you can block the attacker. But you can also ban its IP You can also quarantine its IP address.

- Navigate to policy and objects, **ipv4 DoS policy**
- Create a Dos policy under layer three anomalies or layer four anomalies
- Set up the different thresholds
- Set up the action

One thing is missing, that is to ban or quarantine the IP address of the attacker.

To do so you will need to go to your command line
"config firewall DoS-policy"
"edit 1"
"config anomaly"
"edit <anomaly>
You can move around the different types of anomaliesICMP sweep, the TCP half-open connections, which is actually a SYN that is sent without the ACK, port scanning, and other vulnerabilities that your IPS can actually alert you from.

```
FortiGate-VM64 (1) # config fiFortiGate-VM64 (1) # config fiabort

FortiGate-VM64 # FortiGate-VM64 #
FortiGate-VM64 # config firFortiGate-VM64 # config firewall DoS-policy

FortiGate-VM64 (DoS-policy) # edit 1

FortiGate-VM64 (1) # config anomaly

FortiGate-VM64 (anomaly) # edit icmp_sweep
```

So let's configure the anomaly. Let's set the anomaly to ICMP sweep
Now once you do so, you can actually set the different parameters such as the status, Log, and Do you want to quarantine
The answer is yes, we want to quarantine the attacker

```
FortiGate-VM64 (1) # config fiFortiGate-VM64 (1) # config fiabort

FortiGate-VM64 # FortiGate-VM64 #
FortiGate-VM64 # config firFortiGate-VM64 # config firewall DoS-policy

FortiGate-VM64 (DoS-policy) # edit 1

FortiGate-VM64 (1) # config anomaly

FortiGate-VM64 (anomaly) # edit icmp_sweep

FortiGate-VM64 (icmp_sweep) # set action block

FortiGate-VM64 (icmp_sweep) # set threshold 30

FortiGate-VM64 (icmp_sweep) # set quarantine attacker

FortiGate-VM64 (icmp_sweep) # set quarantine-expiry 1d

FortiGate-VM64 (icmp_sweep) # end
```

"set quarantine attacker"

"set quarantine-expiry" <>

Here it is and we can set it to different time intervals. The default is five minutes, but we can set it to one day, one week, three hours, and so on. So let's set it to one day.

Whenever your IPS sees such an event, it will act upon but it will also ban or quarantine the IP address.

Web Application **Firewall**

Your Fortigate firewall can also protect your network servers, not only your clients.

This means that another approach is needed, as attacks against servers utilize a different kind of vulnerabilities

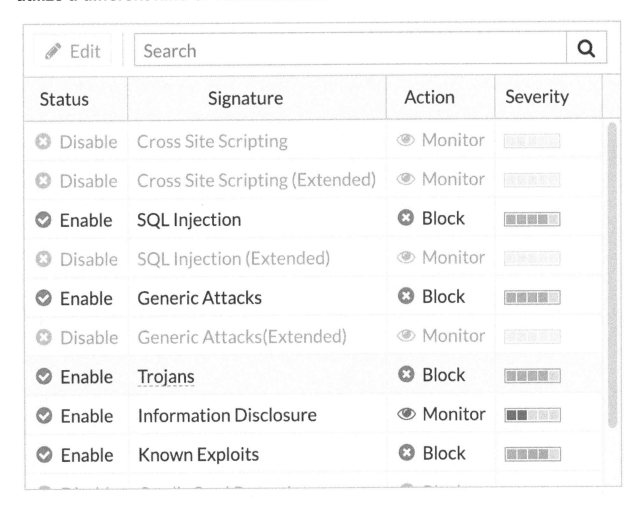

In the case that you need to protect your servers, you can enable the WAF (Web application firewall) on your fortigate.

The WAF security Profile uses the IPS engine, to inspect and recognize malicious attempts

The following scenario is quite typical.

You have a DMZ interface. And behind that, you have your web servers.

Our requirements are as follows:
- We need to create a virtual IP object that will allow only users from the US to enter that webserver. VIP is very similar to port forwarding, you forward a request that is coming to your WAN interface straight to a specific destination inside your LAN
- Only HTTP and HTTPS traffic is allowed
- We will create a web and that is a web application firewall profile for that web server.

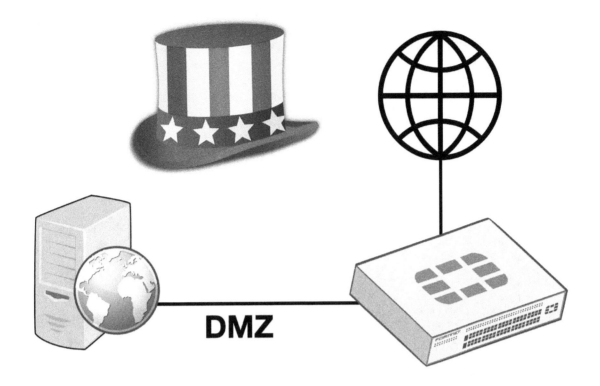

We will start by using one of the free interfaces and create the "webserver" DMZ.

Let's name our interface web server and the role will be DMZ.

Navigate to network-interfaces and double click one of your interfaces

Edit Interface

Name   webserver (port3)

Alias   webserver

Type   Physical Interface

Role 🛈   DMZ ▼

Address

Addressing mode   **Manual**   DHCP   One-Arm Sniffer

IP/Netmask   10.0.6.1/255.255.255.0

Create address object matching subnet ⬤

Secondary IP address ⬤

Administrative access

IPv4
- ☐ HTTPS   ☐ PING   ☐ FMG-Access
- ☐ SSH   ☐ SNMP   ☐ FTM
- ☐ RADIUS Accounting   ☐ Security Fabric Connection 🛈

Receive LLDP 🛈   **Use VDOM Setting**   Enable   Disable

Transmit LLDP 🛈   **Use VDOM Setting**   Enable   Disable

Network

We can also use a LAN role. But the thing behind DMZ is that it actually hides different things from the outside. One of them is the DHCP server.

Now let's create the address itself. Let's make it at the 10.0.6.1/24 we will not enable anything on the administrative access. And that's it.

We have our DMZ, which is at Port 3

The next thing to do is to create a VIP that will allow outside users to get into our web server.

VIP - virtual IP is used to map one IP address to another IP address, also known as destination NAT. very similar to port forwarding on our home router

To create our VIP, navigate to **Policy and object---- virtual IP**

Create a new virtual IP and let's name our VIP **"webserver"**

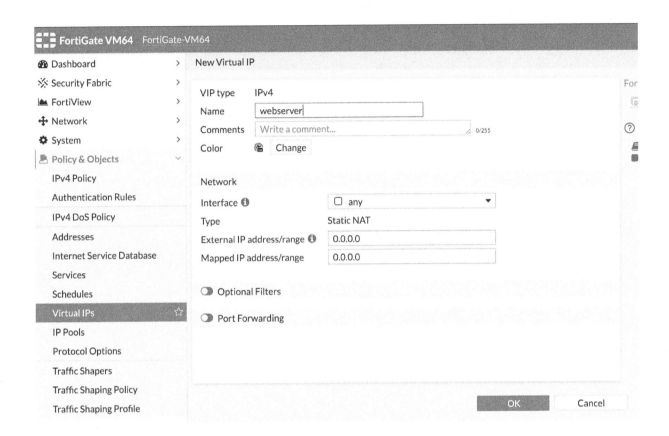

Our external interface will be the WAN interface, 82.33.44.55

let's assume that our web server is at 10.0.6.77 on the 10.0.6.0 subnet we created before

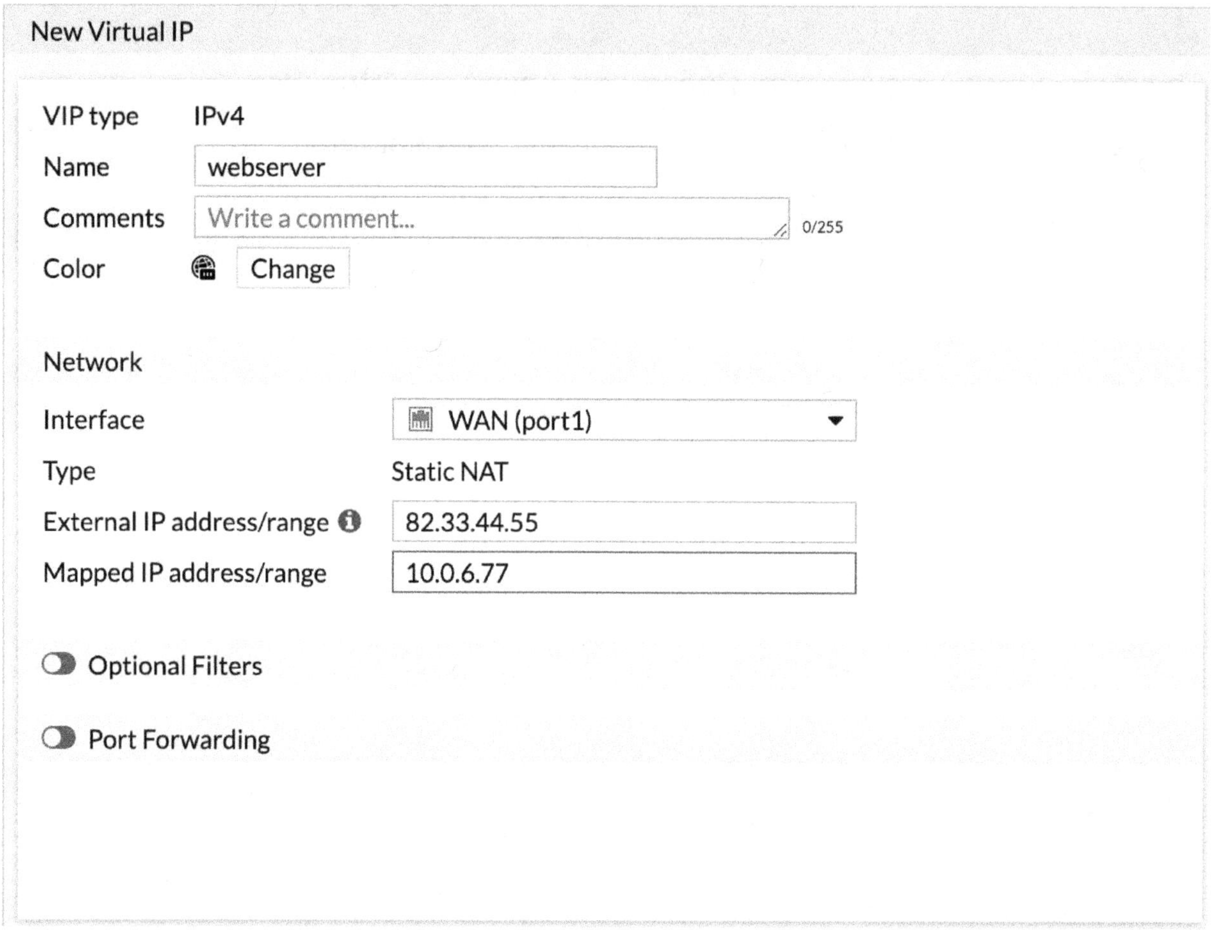

New Virtual IP

VIP type	IPv4
Name	webserver
Comments	Write a comment... 0/255
Color	🌐 Change

Network

Interface	🖳 WAN (port1) ▼
Type	Static NAT
External IP address/range ⓘ	82.33.44.55
Mapped IP address/range	10.0.6.77

◯ Optional Filters

◯ Port Forwarding

The next thing to do is to move to **system -------- feature visibility**

Click **apply** and enable the web application firewall.

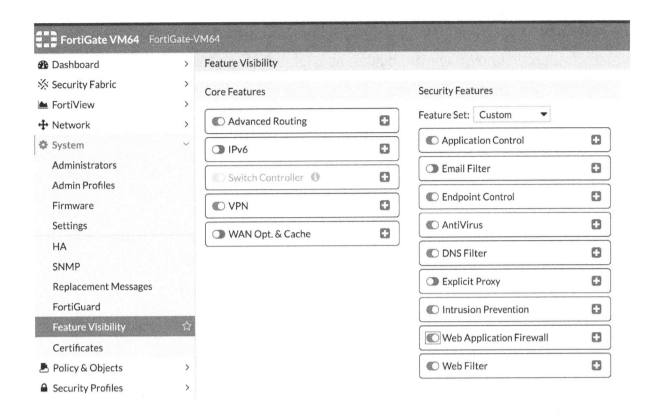

If we move to security profiles. You will see that you a new security profile to configure which is the web application firewall

On your WAF security profile, you can protect your web servers from multiple attacks based on known vulnerabilities as SQL injection, XSS cross-site scripting, buffer overflow, and you can also play around with the HTTP constraints. Choose your settings based on your network needs

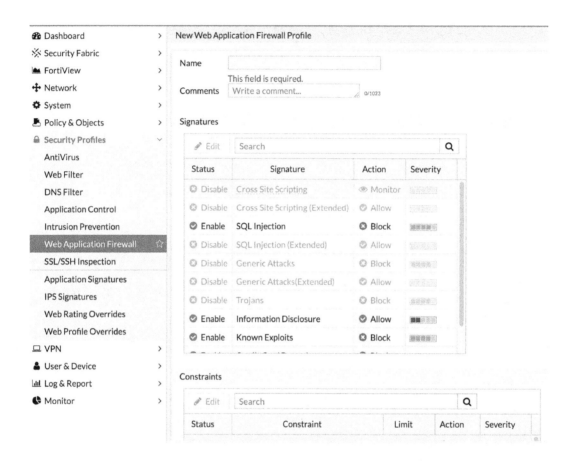

Let's move to our ipv4 policy menu and create a new policy.

Let's name it web server_in.

incoming interfaces- WAN

The outgoing interface is our web server interface, That's our DMZ.

Source - to limit access only to users from the U.S we will create a firewall address object to add up an address that is of type geography. . click on the +Add button to the right of your select entries menu, name your address **U.S_only, type geography, country--united states**

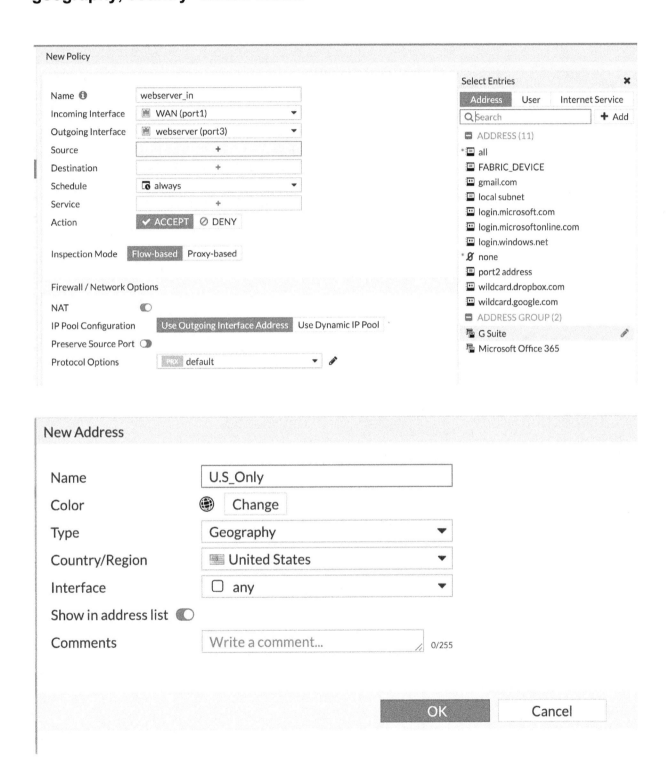

There it is. Okay. And let's just choose that address.

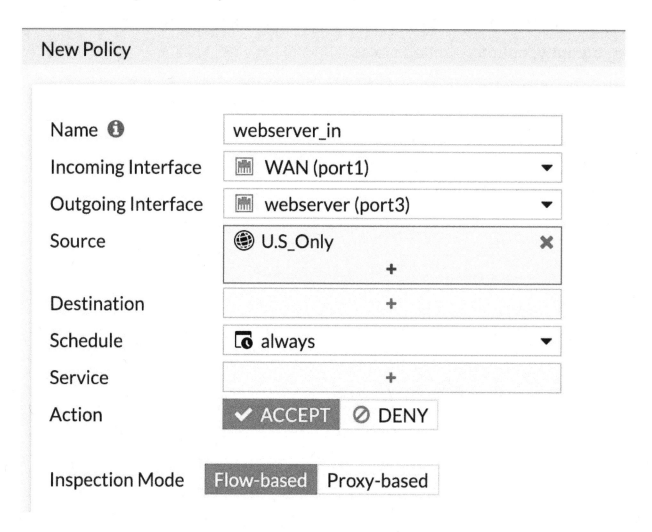

The destination is the VIP that we have created before.

Name ℹ	webserver_in
Incoming Interface	🖧 WAN (port1) ▾
Outgoing Interface	🖧 webserver (port3) ▾
Source	🌐 U.S_Only ✖
	✛
Destination	✛
Schedule	🕓 always ▾
Service	✛
Action	✔ ACCEPT ⊘ DENY
Inspection Mode	Flow-based Proxy-based

Firewall / Network Options

NAT	⬤
IP Pool Configuration	Use Outgoing Interface Addre...
Preserve Source Port	⬤
Protocol Options	default

Security Profiles

Select Entries ✖

Address	Internet Service

🔍 Search　　　　　　 ✚ Create

▢ ADDRESS (12)
* 🖾 all
　🖾 FABRIC_DEVICE
　🖾 gmail.com
　🖾 local subnet
　🖾 login.microsoft.com
　🖾 login.microsoftonline.com
　🖾 login.windows.net
* 🖾 none
　🖾 port2 address
　🌐 U.S_Only
　🖾 wildcard.dropbox.com
　🖾 wildcard.google.com
▢ ADDRESS GROUP (2)
　🖳 G Suite
　🖳 Microsoft Office 365
▢ VIRTUAL IP/SERVER (1)
　🌐 webserver　　　　　🖉

Virtual IP/Server	🌐 webserver
Interface	port1
External IP Address/Range	82.33.44.55
Mapped IP Address/Range	10.0.6.77
References	0
🖉 Edit	

Since we're dealing with a web server, the only two services that are allowed are HTTP and HTTPS.

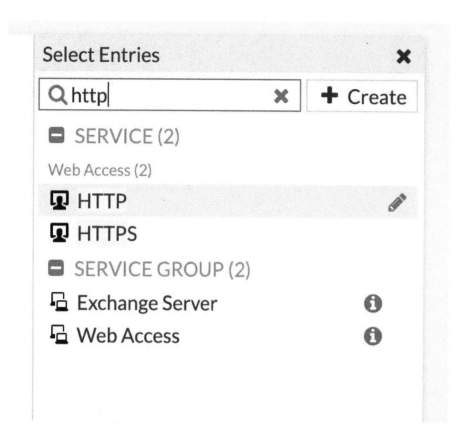

Since we're using a web application firewall, we will need to use the proxy-based inspection mode. And here on our web application firewall, we will use our security profile.

Now the last thing is to disable **NAT**.

Firewall / Network Options

NAT

Protocol Options   PRX   default

We don't really need to use NAT since we already have our VIP object which maps the external IP to the inside private IP

Explicit Proxy

You can configure your fortigate to become a secure web gateway using a proxy. You can use either **Explicit Proxy or Transparent Proxy**.

A web proxy intercepts requests from clients to servers, there are actually 2 TCP connections, that are done

- **From the client to the proxy**
- **From the proxy to the server**

Proxy

Host request   **Proxy request**

Proxies help administrators in creating fewer policies and have greater control on network traffic that is passing through the interfaces, You can also use proxies to apply web authentication to HTTP traffic that is accepted by the firewall policy. there are many things that can be done with a proxy, including web cache, we will focus on the most important configurations

When using an Explicit Proxy, you will need to add up the IP address of the proxy itself, either manually in the browser or using a PAC (**Proxy Auto-Config**) file.

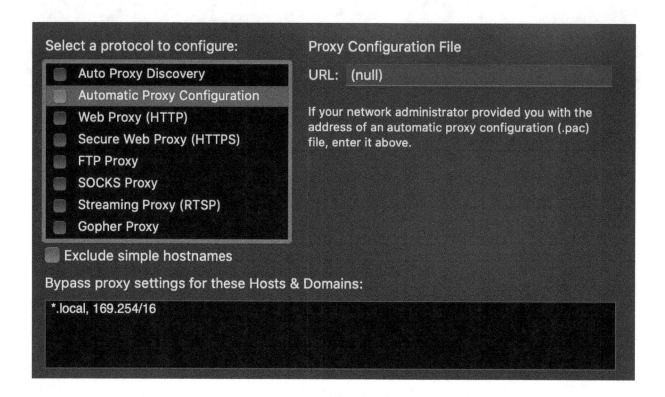

Configuring explicit proxy involves some steps.

The very first thing to enable explicit proxy is navigating to **system --- feature visibility** and make sure that the explicit proxy is enabled.

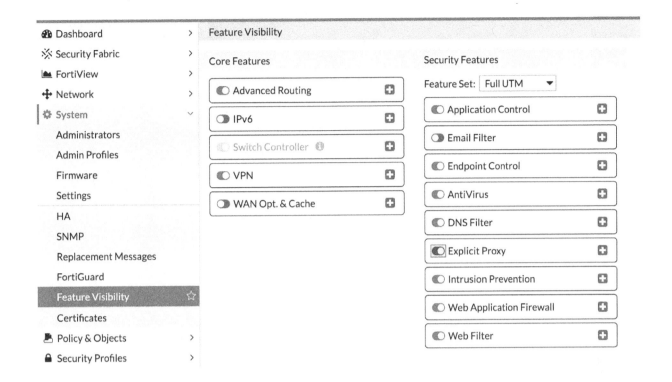

Now move to the interface that you wish to apply the proxy

Move to the bottom of the page and enable Explicit Proxy

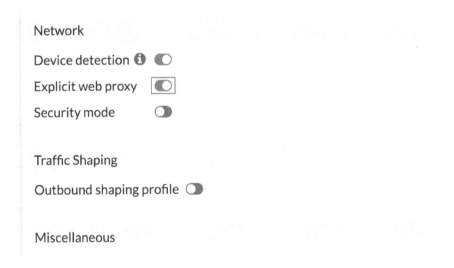

The next thing is to move to network ------ explicit proxy

Enable explicit proxy

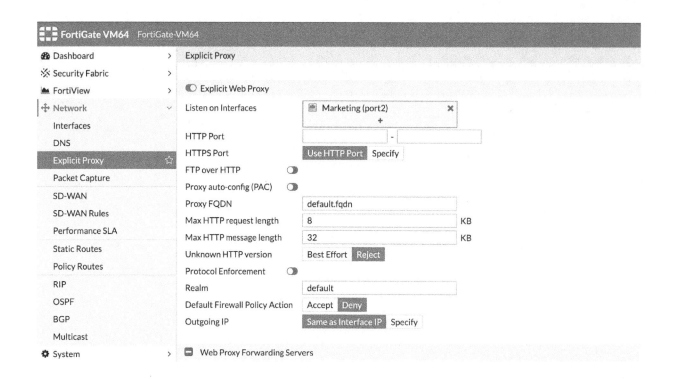

On the explicit proxy page, you will see that it is enabled on our LAN interface (if not, just click the + sign and choose your interface)

The HTTP port is usually 8080, but you can change it if you wish to

Explicit Proxy

Explicit Web Proxy

Listen on Interfaces	Marketing (port2) ✖ +
HTTP Port	8080 - 8080
HTTPS Port	Use HTTP Port Specify
FTP over HTTP	
Proxy auto-config (PAC)	
PAC Port	Use HTTP Port Specify
PAC File Content	✏ Edit ⬇ Download
Proxy FQDN	default.fqdn
Max HTTP request length	8 KB
Max HTTP message length	32 KB
Unknown HTTP version	Best Effort Reject
Protocol Enforcement	
Realm	default
Default Firewall Policy Action	Accept Deny
Outgoing IP	Same as Interface IP Specify

The default setting of your Proxy is set to **Deny**, so change it to **Accept**

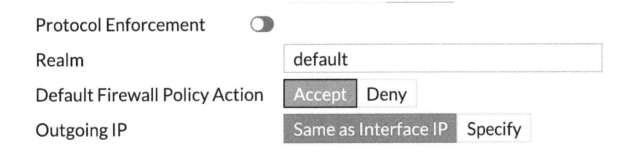

Protocol Enforcement	
Realm	default
Default Firewall Policy Action	Accept Deny
Outgoing IP	Same as Interface IP Specify

Proxy Auto-Config

We can also enable the proxy auto-configuration, which is a text file that contains proxy settings

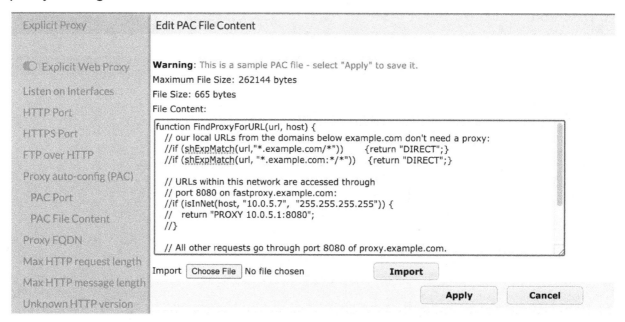

let's just edit the configuration file

We can see that if we have a host, that is at the 10.0.5.7, that's our host that is connected to our marketing LAN (it could also be the full subnet and not only the host)

We redirect our host to the proxy at the **10.0.5.1 in port 8080**

The PAC file has its own URL, you can use your command line
"get web-proxy explicit"

```
CLI Console                                    ●  🗑  ⬇  📄  ↗  ✕

FortiGate-VM64 # get web-proxy explicit
status                : enable
ftp-over-http         : disable
socks                 : disable
http-incoming-port    : 8080
https-incoming-port   :
incoming-ip           : 0.0.0.0
outgoing-ip           :
ipv6-status           : disable
strict-guest          : disable
unknown-http-version: reject
realm                 : default
sec-default-action    : deny
https-replacement-message: enable
message-upon-server-error: enable
pac-file-server-status: enable
pac-file-url          : http://incoming_ip|interface_ip|FGT_FQDN:pac_port/pa
                        Examples: http://192.168.2.1.1:8080/proxy.pac
                                  http://sales_pac.fortigate.com:8080/sales
                                  http://[fe80::eade:27ff:fe04:9a20]:8080/pr

pac-file-server-port:
pac-file-name         : proxy.pac
pac-file-data         : "function FindProxyForURL(url, host) {
--More-- █
```

here you will find the syntax which is:

http:// followed by the address of that interface, the port / proxy.pac

```
pac-file-url             : http://incoming_ip|interface_ip|FGT_FQDN:pac_port/
                           Examples: http://192.168.2.1.1:8080/proxy.pac
```

We need to enter that at the proxy configuration in our browser

Proxy Configuration File

URL: (null)

If your network administrator provided you with the address of an automatic proxy configuration (.pac) file, enter it above.

let's move to policy & objects ---- proxy policy.

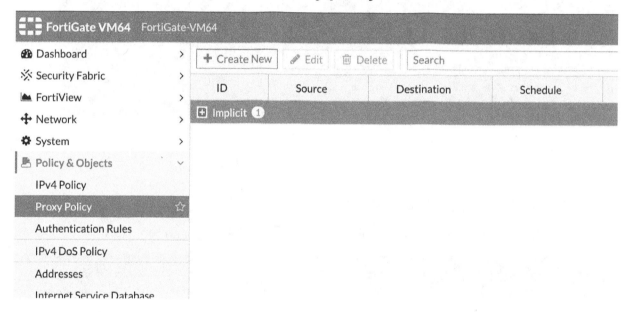

Create New

we can see that we have an Explicit web proxy policy enabled on port two

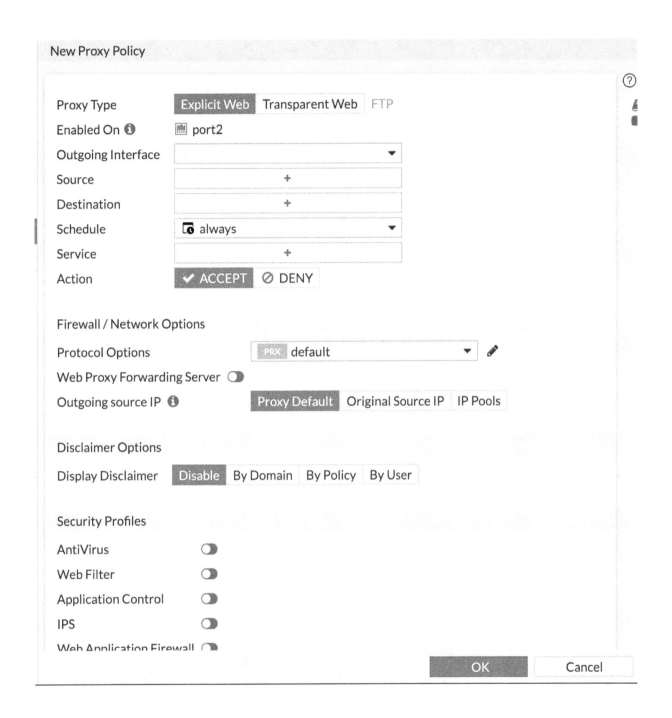

The outgoing Interface is our WAN interface

- Source - All we will enable it to all users without any credentials
- Destination - ALL
- Schedule - Always
- Service is web proxy

Our First match should look like that:

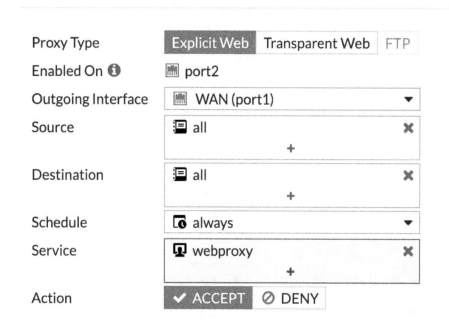

Next, you can apply security profiles the same as you would do on any other policy.

Security Profiles

AntiVirus　　　　　　　⬤○

Web Filter　　　　　　　⬤○

Application Control　　○⬤　| APP default ▼ | ✎

IPS　　　　　　　　　　| ○⬤ | | IPS default ▼ | ✎

Web Application Firewall ⬤○

SSL Inspection　　　　　　　　　| SSL certificate-inspection ▼ | ✎

Logging Options

Log Allowed Traffic ○⬤ | Security Events | All Sessions |

Comments　　| Write a comment... | 0/1023

| OK | | Cancel |

And that's the **basic configuration** of an Explicit proxy. You can set many more advanced settings related to authentication and network

Block IP Domains

There are times when you are asked to block a list of domains, that are related to applications, that may cause harm to your network

As long as you control the connection which users connect to those apps, you can try to block access to the app at the **DNS** level, using a block list of IP's and domains that are related to that app

In our example, we will try to block the TikTok app, but this could be any app. The concept is the same

The first thing you will need to do is to get hold of TikTok domains and IP's

TikTok uses different domains where it connects to when users log in, upload, or view videos. to cut that, you will need to google **"block TikTok domains"**

G✦gle block tiktok domains   ✕ 🎤 🔍

🔍 All   🖼 Images   ▶ Videos   📰 News   ⌖ Maps   ⋮ More   Settings   Tools

About 1,130,000 results (0.67 seconds)

Here is the list of TikTok app domain names which you need to block in web content filtering:

1. v16a.tiktokcdn.com.
2. p16-tiktokcdn-com.akamaized.net.
3. log.tiktokv.com.
4. ib.tiktokv.com.
5. api-h2.tiktokv.com.
6. v16m.tiktokcdn.com.
7. api.tiktokv.com.
8. v19.tiktokcdn.com.

More items... • Dec 29, 2019

www.digitbin.com › Tech Tips   traffic (us): 44/mo - keywords (us): 8
How to Block TikTok on WiFi Network Router? - DigitBin

                                        ❓ About Featured Snippets   🏴 Feedback

Now copy all the domains and paste them into a text file and save it

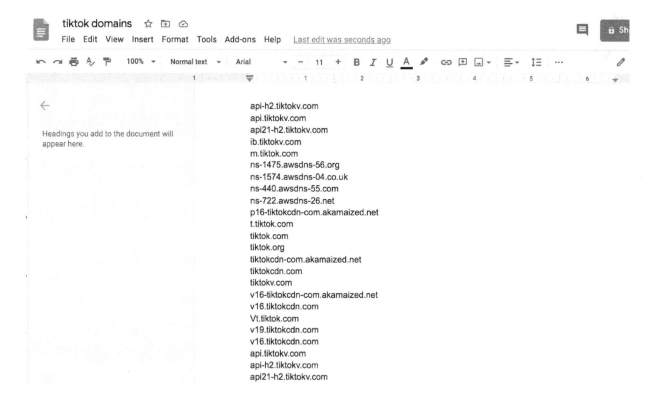

Headings you add to the document will appear here.

```
api-h2.tiktokv.com
api.tiktokv.com
api21-h2.tiktokv.com
ib.tiktokv.com
m.tiktok.com
ns-1475.awsdns-56.org
ns-1574.awsdns-04.co.uk
ns-440.awsdns-55.com
ns-722.awsdns-26.net
p16-tiktokcdn-com.akamaized.net
t.tiktok.com
tiktok.com
tiktok.org
tiktokcdn-com.akamaized.net
tiktokcdn.com
tiktokv.com
v16-tiktokcdn-com.akamaized.net
v16.tiktokcdn.com
Vt.tiktok.com
v19.tiktokcdn.com
v16.tiktokcdn.com
api.tiktokv.com
api-h2.tiktokv.com
api21-h2.tiktokv.com
```

The file should be plain text with one IP address on each line

On our FortiGate firewall, we will use an **External IP block list**, in many other devices, you could probably enter the list manually, but here we will actually load our text file to a web server so that we could manage the list more easily as we may need to add more domains

Log into your **FortiGate-security fabric — -fabric connectors** . that is the place where we will connect to the list of TikTok IP's

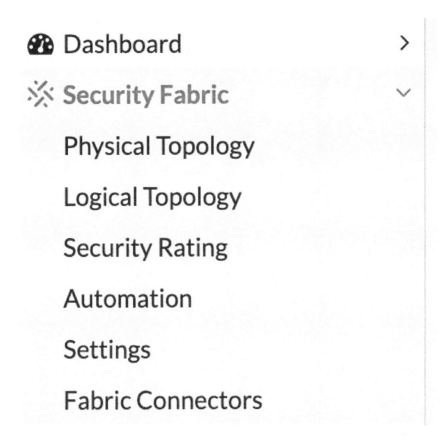

Once opened, click on the create new, and you will see the following page

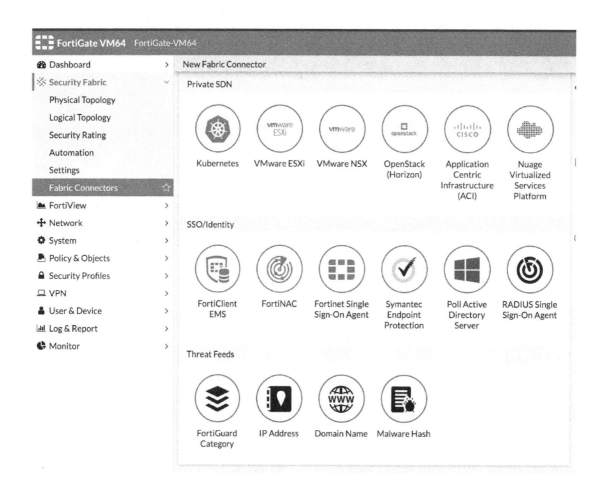

There are different connectors, but we will choose the threat feeds connector at the bottom of the page and choose the IP address

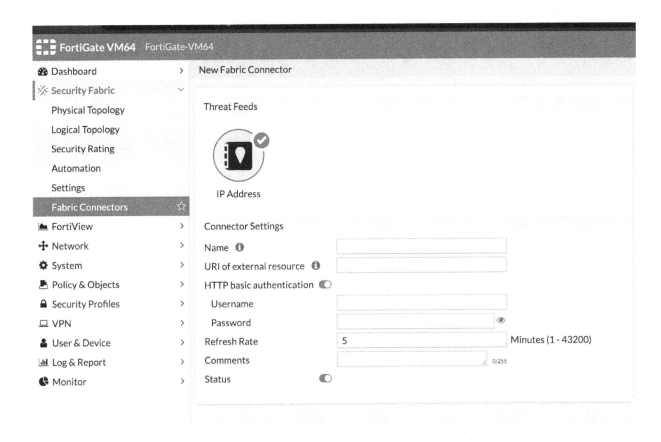

Name your threat feed and Enter your text path

Threat Feeds

IP Address

Connector Settings

Name ⓘ	TikTok domains
URI of external resource ⓘ	https://88.2.3.4
HTTP basic authentication 🔘	
Username	
Password	👁
Refresh Rate	5 Minutes (1 - 43200)
Comments	0/255
Status 🔘	

Once saved, you will see your first threat feed

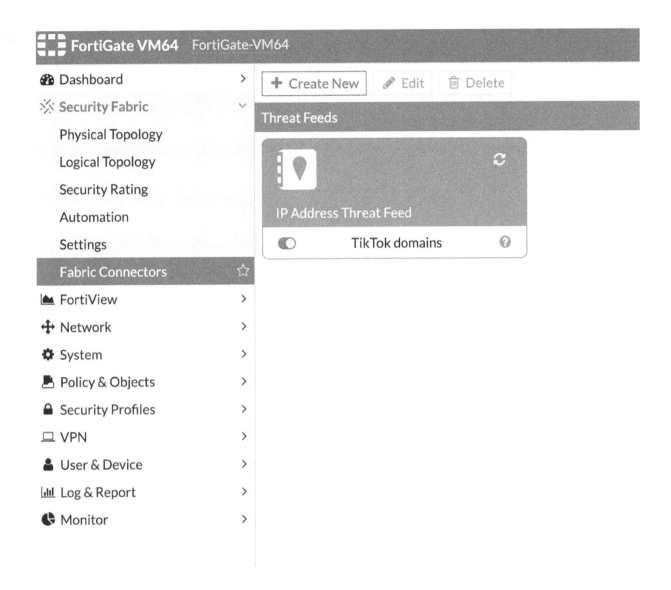

Let's move to our DNS filter, which is located at the security profiles pane

🔒 Security Profiles ⌄

AntiVirus

Web Filter

DNS Filter

Application Control

Intrusion Prevention

SSL/SSH Inspection

Application Signatures

Click and create a new DNS filter sensor and name it **"Block TikTok"**

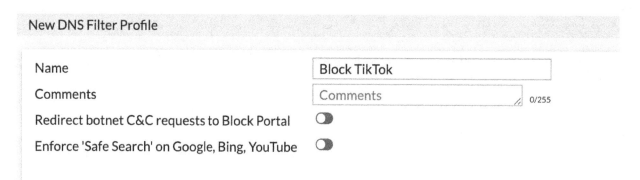

Scroll down to the static domain filter part

Enable it

Static Domain Filter

Domain Filter

External IP Block Lists   +

DNS Translation ℹ️

Press the **+ sign** and choose the entries, your threat feed (the one you created before in the fabric connectors)

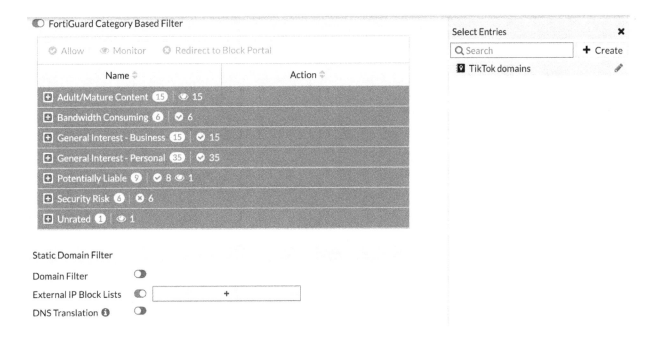

Click OK and save it

On your DNS filter page, you will see your new filter

Let's move to the final part, apply your DNS filter to your Policy

Now Move to policy and objects — -IPV4 policy

And click on the policy, you want to add the DNS filter, in my case it is the full access policy

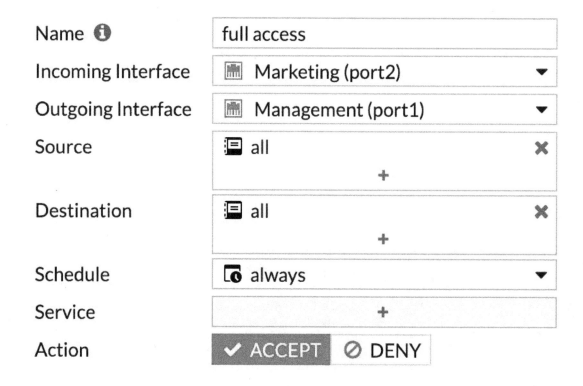

Scroll down to the security profiles part

Enable the DNS filter and choose our **Block TikTok Filter**

Security Profiles

AntiVirus

Web Filter

DNS Filter

| DNS | default | ▼ | 🖊 |

| 🔍 Search | | **+** Create | 🖊 |

| DNS | **block TikTok** | 🖊 |
| DNS | default | |

Application Control

IPS

SSL Inspection 🖊

Save your Policy, and you're **Done**

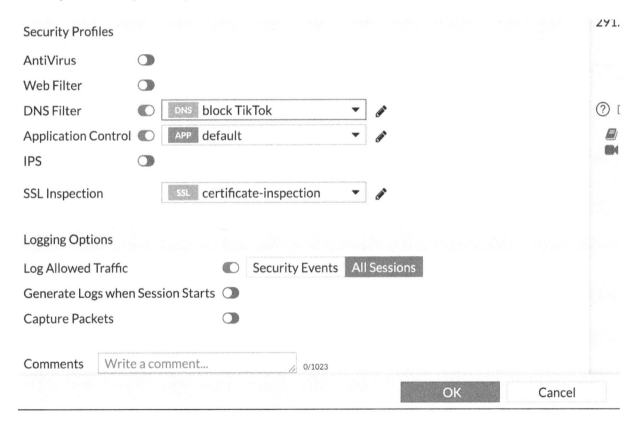

Security Profiles

AntiVirus

Web Filter

DNS Filter | DNS | block TikTok | ▼ | 🖊 |

Application Control | APP | default | ▼ | 🖊 |

IPS

SSL Inspection | SSL | certificate-inspection | ▼ | 🖊 |

Logging Options

Log Allowed Traffic   Security Events | All Sessions

Generate Logs when Session Starts

Capture Packets

Comments | Write a comment... | 0/1023

| **OK** | Cancel |

Final **Words**

You have just Finished "Fortigate Security Pocket Guide " Part 2

I hope that you enjoyed the journey. My aim was to give you a head start on security profiles, and how to protect your network, on one of the best next-generation firewalls in the market.

Sincerely yours

Ofer Shmueli